T5-DHH-333

I'm Glad You Know Where We're Going, Lord

Books by Andrea and Bill Stephens

Stressed Out but Hangin' Tough
Prime Time: Devotions for Girls
Prime Time: Devotions for Guys
Ready for Prime Time: Devotions for Girls
Ready for Prime Time: Devotions for Guys

I'm Glad You Know Where We're Going, Lord

*Andrea and
Bill Stephens*

Fleming H. Revell
A Division of Baker Book House Co
Grand Rapids, Michigan 49516

©1996 by Andrea and Bill Stephens

Published by Fleming H. Revell
a division of Baker Book House Company
P.O. Box 6287, Grand Rapids, MI 49516-6287

Printed in the United States of America

All rights reserved. No part of this publication may be reproduced, stored in a retrieval system, or transmitted in any form or by any means—for example, electronic, photocopy, recording—without the prior written permission of the publisher. The only exception is brief quotations in printed reviews.

Library of Congress Cataloging-in-Publication Data

Stephens, Andrea, 1959-
    I'm glad you know where we're going, Lord / Andrea and Bill Stephens.
       p.   cm.
    Summary : A devotional designed to help the reader discover and follow God's plan for one's life.
    ISBN 0-8007-5599-5 (paper)
    1. Teenagers—Prayer-books and devotions—English. 2. Spiritual life—Christianity—Juvenile literature. [1. Prayer books and devotions. 2. Christian life.] I. Stephens, Bill, 1957-   . II. Title. III. Title: I'm glad you know where we're going, Lord
BV4531.2.S75   1996
248.8'3—dc20   96-3209

Unless otherwise indicated, Scripture is taken from *The Living Bible*, copyright © 1971 by Tyndale House Publishers, Wheaton, Illinois. Used by permission.

Scripture quotations marked NASB are taken from the New American Standard Bible, © the Lockman Foundation 1960, 1962, 1963, 1968, 1971, 1972, 1973, 1975, 1977.

Other versions cited are New International Version (NIV), King James Version (KJV), and Amplified Bible (AMP).

HERE'S
WHAT'S
INCLUDED!

This book is dedicated to

Betty Garrett, a trusted friend
who has helped me (Andrea) find
the Lord's direction in my life over the years

Rowena Glessner, who prayed
with me (Bill) in 1970 to begin
the Christian journey

Our precious parents,
Nell Stephens and the late Bill Stephens,
R. J. and Joanne Ardner
We appreciate your continued guidance.

Our readers
May God grant you the ability to see the joy
in following him on your journey through life.

ACKNOWLEDGMENTS

Thanks a lot!

To Francie, for looking up all these Scriptures and for your never-ending support.

To Kristin, for reading the manuscript from a young adult's perspective.

To Lynda, for having the patience to type and retype!

To our family and our friends at Covington Presbyterian Church who prayed for us during this project!

To our friends at Revell. Thanks for believing in our books and helping to meet the needs of teens.

To Bob and Flora, for the week at your beachfront condo. It gave us a great jump start into organizing our thoughts.

To my (Andrea's) Bible study buddies who listened to me when I was brain-dead and tired of writing! It's finally done! Let's do lunch!

INTRODUCTION

HOW TO READ THESE ROAD SIGNS

Get the map! Oil your wheels! Load up your backpack! You are about to take off on an exciting journey! *I'm Glad You Know Where We're Going, Lord* will help you begin to understand God's plan as you travel through life. You will learn that through a close relationship with Jesus and an increased knowledge of the Bible, you *can* hear his voice; you can detect his leading. It will take effort on your part. God doesn't send telegrams or faxes. You won't find a message in your e-mail or on your answering machine.

Our book is designed as a devotional. The first two chapters will get you geared up to dig into the next nine! Chapters 3 through 11 include five daily readings. Each day stands on its own, though it relates to the topic of the week. Each day also contains two parts: the beginning will usually be a story that illustrates the main point of the day, and the second part, subtitled "Rest Stop, Exit Here" provides an opportunity for you to pull off the road for a minute.

Don't cheat yourself by skipping the "Rest Stops." These sections will help you dig deeper into the Scriptures and think through the main points and see how to apply them to your life. Because you need God's direction every day, you'll be able to start putting these principles into practice right away! We couldn't include every single detail about discovering God's will for your life, of course, but you will definitely be given a firm foundation to launch your investigation into God's plan.

As you travel with God, seeking his direction for your life, our prayer for you is not that God will make the road before you smooth and easy. Instead, we'll be praying for him to make you strong and wise to endure whatever the road before you brings.

There will be sharp turns, road blocks, thunderstorms, deserts, mountaintops, cliffs, dead ends, potholes, steep uphill climbs, and some fun downhill cruises!

No matter the road, rest assured, you never travel alone. With the Bible as your map and the Holy Spirit as your guiding light, God, your Heavenly Father, will direct you, his precious child. Go ahead. Take his hand. Follow his lead!

P.S. If you're new to this study stuff, let us clue you in. Choose a special time each day to do your devotions. Studying at the same time each day will help get you into a pattern. Begin with prayer. Ask God to open your heart and mind to his truths. After your study time, close in prayer. Pray for wisdom to apply what you've learned, then pray for other needs in your life as well.

As you go through the book you'll see Bible references followed by some capital letters such as 1 Timothy 4:12 NASB. That refers to the first letter to Timothy, chapter four, verse twelve. The letters refer to the version of the Bible. NASB = New American Standard Bible, NIV = New International Version, KJV = King James Version. Most of the Bible quotations in this book are from *The Living Bible,* so if no abbreviation follows the Bible reference, it's from that version. You can read the verse in whatever version you have, though at some point you might like to have more than one version.

Let's get started!

THE SCENIC OVERLOOK

The Big Picture from God's Point of View

Andrea

Bill was Mr. Romance early in our dating life. He poured on the charm trying to woo me (you guys are like that, you know)! On our second date, Bill planned a picnic at the lake. He packed the hot dogs, drinks, potato chips, and all the fixin's—even remembered the blanket to sit on (no charcoal, though; he used the ol' "rub the sticks together" trick—boy, was he trying to impress me).

After a wonderful dinner of burned wieners under the stars, we headed home. On the way, we pulled over (don't get excited) to check out the sights. They were guaranteed to be grandiose, according to the scenic overview sign: a night view of the city lights reflecting on the flowing ripples of the lake.

Bill was far more into it than I was. He climbed over the protective railing and proceeded to lean way out over the edge of the overhang. We're talking cliff here!

Now, I'm not adventurous, and Bill was beginning to sense it. Though he tried, he was unable to coax me over the railing. I was lagging back, hugging a boulder, totally unnerved. I didn't want to accidentally slip off the edge and fall to my doom (hey, I saw *The Lion King*, I know what can happen). I was totally satisfied with just a peek at the view. Better yet, buy me a postcard! You think I sound like a chicken, don't you? Well, I am! And I accept the fact that I'm a chicken. But that's another story.

Back to the view.

Just to please my newfound prince, I did venture to the railing. I even sat up on it. He was right. I could see for miles way up there. A bird's-eye view. Down the lake and up the lake! Panorama perfection!

God's view is like that. From where he sits, he can see our entire lives. He sees the past, present, and future. He already knows his plans for us up ahead. God sees the BIG PICTURE!

We, however, only get to see our lives piece by piece. We see in part, one step at a time. Yet be assured that God has a plan for your life. He has a will for you and he wants you in it!

During the teen years, questions about identity begin to surface: Who am I? What am I here for? Does life have a meaning, a purpose? What does God want from me? What does he want me to do with my life? These are important questions. It's even more important that you get the answers!

Does God have a plan, a will, a direction for you? Yes! The Bible tells us that God made us and designed us! He scheduled each day of our lives before we were even born (Psalm 139:13–16). Yeah, that's great! But how can you know what his plan is?

That's what this book is all about! See, God's will is in two parts. He has a general will for all of his children that he clearly lays out in his Word (the Bible). Then he has a specific will, just for you. His specific will is for the *major* things in your life. God really doesn't care if you snarf down a pizza or a taco for lunch today, but the biggies do matter to him.

Throughout these pages, we're going to touch on both: general and specific. We'll highlight some of the major "general will" topics that you absolutely need to know (of course, you need to know *all* of them, but we'll get you started). These are things God tells us right up front. These are absolutes. No-foolin'-around-type things. These apply to *all* his kids.

For instance, you'll be wasting your words if you're wrestling with God over whether or not it's okay if you sleep with your steady girlfriend or boyfriend. All the rationale in the world won't change the fact that God has already laid out his guidelines for premarital sex in his Word. His answer? NO.

We will also give some valuable tips on discovering God's direction on the specific things. With God as your travel guide, the Bible as your map, and the Holy Spirit whispering in your ear, you can learn to tune in to sense God's leading in every area of your life. But don't expect God to reveal your whole life to you all at once. It doesn't work that way!

God unrolls his specific plan like a scroll. He shows us bits at a time and at the right time. He'll tell you what you need to know for the moment. He doesn't lay it out all at once.

In an interview with *Campus Life* magazine, Amy Grant said she is shocked over her success. When she was playing her guitar in the living room or in a coffeehouse, God never showed her that she'd be a superstar one day. He led her one step at a time. God may reveal his will for the next day, next month, next year. Hey, sometimes he gives us a glimpse of a few years down the road, but that's about it!

Why does he do it that way? He has his reasons! One reason is that he loves you. He wants what is best for you. If he showed you everything all at once, it might freak you out! Another reason is that he is working on you. He may not show you what to do or answer your request immediately because he's taking you through a learning process of some sort. He's preparing your heart so you'll be ready to accept his plan when he shows you. While I was modeling in New York, if God had suddenly told me I was going to be a pastor's wife instead of gracing the covers of magazines or up on the "Big Screen," I wouldn't have taken it very well. Instead, in his wisdom and gentleness, he showed me the true value of life and convinced me I had more to give this world than a smile on a magazine cover! He did this *before* he told me to pack my bags and head home for the new life he had planned.

Another reason God unfolds his plan for us piece by piece is that it forces us to stay tight with him. Oh, how he longs for us to come to him, to be in his presence. He loves to be with us. It's when we're tuned in that we can hear him speak. And trust me, he cares about you and does have a plan for your life, even now as a teen. Check out how God worked in the young lives of Jeremiah, Samuel, and Timothy (Jeremiah 1:6–7; 1 Samuel 3; 1 Timothy 4:12).

As you travel the road of life, with all its twists and turns, rough bumps and smooth spots, remember—you do not travel alone. The Lord is always with you. In that, you can have peace and confidence.

Bill often closes our church service with these words:

May the Lord go before
    you to lead you,
Behind you to encour-
    age you,
Beside you to befriend
    you,
And within you to give
    you hope and
    strength.

That is our prayer for you, too!

(For Your Information)

I will instruct you (says the Lord) and guide you along the best pathway for your life; I will advise you and watch your progress.

Psalm 32:8

And I am sure that God who began the good work within you will keep right on helping you grow in his grace until his task within you is finally finished on that day when Jesus Christ returns.

Philippians 1:6

For God is at work within you, helping you want to obey him, and then helping you do what he wants.

Philippians 2:13

I am the Lord your God, who teaches you to profit,
Who leads you in the way you should go.

Isaiah 48:17 NASB

And be sure of this—that I am with you always, even to the end of the world.

Matthew 28:20b

You saw me before I was born and scheduled each day of my life before I began to breathe. Every day was recorded in your Book!

Psalm 139:16

Thou wilt make known to me the path of life;
In Thy presence is fulness of joy;
In Thy right hand there are pleasures forever.

Psalm 16:11 NASB

FIRST THINGS FIRST

Before You Begin
the Journey

Andrea

I love to read in bed at night before I go to sleep. Snuggling down into the covers with a good book relaxes me. Bill, on the other hand, doesn't need to "relax." When his head hits the pillow, it's snoozeville for him. He does have one requirement, however; the lights have to be OFF.

Well, it's a little hard for me to read by the light of the moonbeams shining through our miniblinds. The answer? A little book light. Mine has a very sensitive switch; I finally get it turned on, then one tiny tap and it's off! Very moody thing. So I try to motionlessly turn the pages, oh, so carefully. But to no avail. Off it goes again!

Reading in the dark is no good. I can't see the words (or the book for that matter). I can't understand the meaning. I don't get a thing out of it!

Going to church and reading the Bible can be just like that for a person who doesn't have Jesus. The pastor's message, Sunday school class—it doesn't click with them. It's over their head, in one ear and out the other. They may

God's Overall Will for You

- To Become Christlike by Developing the Character of Jesus
  Romans 8:29

- To Glorify God in What You Do and Say
  1 Corinthians 6:20
  Colossians 3:17

- To Tell Others How to Become Part of God's Family
  Matthew 28:18–20

attempt to read the Bible, but the yawns set in. Boring. Pointless. They have no interest in God.

What's the deal? They are in darkness. The light is not on!

The Bible explains that a person who isn't a Christian cannot understand or accept the teachings and thoughts of the Spirit of God. They sound foolish to him. Why? Because only those people who have the Holy Spirit within them can really understand spiritual things (1 Corinthians 2:14).

Marcus shared that he would try to read the Bible his grandma had given to him for his birthday. Yet nothing seemed to make sense. It was lifeless and dull. But once he prayed with his youth pastor to receive Jesus into his heart and to become part of God's family, things changed.

What happened to Marcus happens to everyone who becomes a Christian. They become a new creation; they are reborn on the inside. And better yet, the Holy Spirit *himself* comes to live inside of them!

Let's get some proof from God's Word. Listen to what Jesus told the Jewish leader, Nicodemus:

> Truly, truly, I say to you, unless one is born of water and the Spirit, he cannot enter into the kingdom of God. That which is born of the flesh is flesh, and that which is born of the Spirit is spirit. Do not marvel that I said to you, "You must be born again."
>
> John 3:5–7 NASB

Of course, it's not the body that gets reborn! It's the spirit. When a person prays and asks Jesus to forgive his sins and come into his heart, the Lord sends the Holy Spirit to live right inside of that person.

Jesus told the disciples:

> And I will ask the Father, and He will give you another Helper, that He may be with you forever; *that is* the

Spirit of truth, whom the world cannot receive, because it does not behold Him or know Him, *but* you
know Him because He abides with you, and will be
in you.

John 14:16–17 NASB

The Holy Spirit comes to live inside of believers. One
of the main jobs of the Spirit is to teach us and guide us.
That's great news for discovering God's will. We have a res-
ident teacher that is 100 percent plugged into God!

In fact, Scripture tells us that the Holy Spirit alone knows
the thoughts of God. When we have received the Holy
Spirit, he can reveal God's thoughts and directions to us as
God wills it (1 Corinthians 2:10–12).

When you accept Christ, you have already fulfilled a
major portion of God's plan for your life: to be his child,
part of his family. Now you've started the journey of life
with the Lord. Spiritual things start to make sense. The
Bible becomes your handbook to life. The lights finally
come on!

Are you in the dark or the light? It will be very difficult
to read this book and make an effort to discover God's direction for your life if you are in the dark. Only when you are
his child will you be able to hear his voice!

Why not pray with us to be sure you are in the light, full
of the Holy Spirit and walking this road with the Lord?

Dear Heavenly Father, I believe that you are God, the
Creator of all things, including me. I believe that your Son
Jesus died and was raised from the dead to provide for-
giveness of sin. I know I have sinned. So I ask that you,
Jesus, would forgive me. I want you to come into my life
to be my Lord and Savior. I open the door of my heart
and let you in. Thank you for giving me eternal life. Holy
Spirit, help me to understand spiritual truths. Help me to

hear the Father's voice. Guide me to do his will in my life. Keep me in the light, that I might honor and please him in all I do.

In Jesus' name I pray, Amen.

Welcome to the Family!

(For Your
Information)

For if you tell others with your own mouth that Jesus Christ is your Lord, and believe in your own heart that God has raised him from the dead, you will be saved.

Romans 10:9

You are controlled by your new nature if you have the Spirit of God living in you. (And remember that if anyone doesn't have the Spirit of Christ living in him, he is not a Christian at all.)

Romans 8:9

But when He, the Spirit of truth, comes, He will guide you into all the truth.

John 16:13 NASB

I can *never* be lost to your Spirit! I can *never* get away from my God . . . your hand will guide me, your strength will support me.

Psalm 139: 7, 10

For He delivered us from the domain of darkness, and transferred us to the kingdom of His beloved Son.

Colossians 1:13 NASB

God is light, and in Him there is no darkness at all.

1 John 1:5 NASB

When you meet someone, the first
thing you ask is their name. Since you'll
be traveling with the Trinity, you need
to know their names!

TRAVEL TIPS

There are various names the Bible uses to
refer to God, Jesus, and the Holy Spirit.

These different ways of describing them give
us insight into their purpose and character. Here
are a few of those names.

Introducing . . . God!

Holy Father   Almighty
Creator   Righteous Judge
Most High   Forgiving God

Introducing . . . Jesus!

Savior   King of Kings
Prince of Peace   Wonderful Counselor
Good Shepherd   Friend

Introducing . . . The Holy Spirit!

Comforter   Teacher
Helper   Voice of the Lord
Spirit of Truth   Power

LEARNING TO MANEUVER THE MAP

God's Word—the Key to a Successful Trip!

DAY ONE
Mapping Out God's General Will

Andrea

The Great Escape: good title for a rowdy junior high youth camp. I had been invited to speak to the girls during the morning sessions of camp. The second day, right before all seven hundred girls were due to flood into the chapel, a husky seventh grade boy with curly hair and glasses came wandering in. I looked up as he made his way down the center aisle. Being polite even while I panicked (I knew he didn't belong in there, he wasn't a girl!), I asked, "Can I help you?"

He looked up at me sheepishly and said, "I don't know what I'm doing here." At first, I thought, *Well, I don't either; guys are supposed to meet in the cafeteria.* Sensing he meant something different, I took a shot. "You mean you don't know what you're doing at camp?"

"No," he replied, looking at me like I was very slow of mind. "I don't know what I'm doing here on earth. I don't know what I'm here for."

Oh! The identity crisis! What's my purpose? What's the meaning of life? What does God want for me and from me? The BIG questions!

Thanks, Lord, I grumbled in my mind. *You're giving me all of four minutes to explain the purpose of life to this searching young man!*

It's a fact that the teen years bring with them many puzzling questions. Let me assure you God has a plan for you and he wants to reveal it to you. God's not into hide 'n' seek. It's not a game. In fact, God's will for your life is clearly laid out in his Word.

The Bible contains God's general will for all Christians. His Word is filled with guidelines for your life. This is God's main way of communicating with us. There are some do's, like: Go into all the world and share the gospel (from Mark 16:15). That tells us it is God's will for us to tell others about Jesus. There are also some don'ts, like: Don't be teamed together with people who do not love the Lord (from 2 Corinthians 6:14). This can apply to dating life, telling us to only date and marry someone who honors God like you do. Both do's and don'ts are radically important!

God's Word is full of guidelines to help us find our way. They are beacons of light shining on his path for us to follow.

You can know God's general will for your life by studying the map, the Bible. In fact, the studying of God's Word will give you a solid foundation for the decisions and choices that you'll have to make. Are you willing?

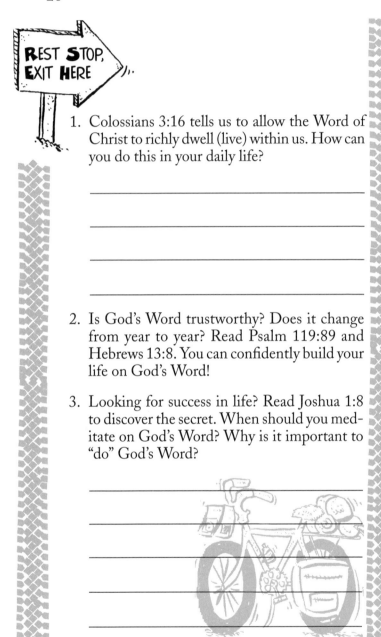

REST STOP, EXIT HERE

1. Colossians 3:16 tells us to allow the Word of Christ to richly dwell (live) within us. How can you do this in your daily life?

_____

_____

_____

_____

2. Is God's Word trustworthy? Does it change from year to year? Read Psalm 119:89 and Hebrews 13:8. You can confidently build your life on God's Word!

3. Looking for success in life? Read Joshua 1:8 to discover the secret. When should you meditate on God's Word? Why is it important to "do" God's Word?

_____

_____

_____

_____

_____

DAY TWO
How Do You Read This Dusty Old Thing?

Bill

There are some who say I have a reputation for getting lost. I earned this reputation by never taking a map along on youth group trips. I figured as long as I knew the general direction I could find my way.

One summer I was driving a vanload of junior high students to Hume Lake summer camp in central California. Just east of Fresno are miles and miles of orange groves we needed to travel through before starting up into the mountains. As I guessed my way along the kids chattered behind me, unaware that I was once again lost. I knew there was only one road, Highway 180, that led up into the mountains and to the camp, but I couldn't find it. After a half hour of searching I finally stopped at a house to ask directions and we found the correct route. When we arrived at camp, we were late for dinner and the kids were upset with me. On top of this, I had used up lots of extra gas and precious time. Next time, I promised them I would bring a map!

The same thing happens in our spiritual lives if we don't read the Bible; it is our map! God gave it to us to steer us through storms and to warn us about bends in the road. It is our *handbook* to life. But if we leave it unread on our nightstand or on the bottom of our bookshelves or under the bed beneath last week's wrinkled wardrobe, it *can't* be the guiding light God intends for it to be.

I can hear your brain cranking out those typical ol' excuses. I've heard them from tons of teens: "The Bible is old;

In This Best-Selling Book of All Time, You Will Find:

Love, Adventure, War, Tragedy, Joy, Celebrations, Drama, Humor, History, Wickedness, Satanic Oppression, Glory, Hope

Whoever Said the Bible Was Boring?

it doesn't relate to *my* life." "I can't understand it." "It doesn't apply to me." "I can't even pronounce those names and places . . ."

Oh, quit! No more excuses! The Bible won't read itself, but it doesn't take a genius to figure it out. Of course, it will help if you get a version of the Bible that has language that is easy to understand, like *The Living Bible* or a student Bible.

The fact that there are different versions does not mean the content is different, simply that the same things are said in different ways.

For instance, let's read Proverbs 19:20 from the King James Version: "Hear counsel, and receive instruction, that thou mayest be wise in thy latter end."

Now check out the same verse from *The Living Bible:* "Get all the advice you can and be wise the rest of your life."

Big difference, huh! They say exactly the same thing, yet one is in words that make it easier to catch the meaning.

When you're selecting the version you can understand best, you may want to look at the Bibles that have built-in study guides. That's an extra bonus. Those footnotes allow you to read up on meanings and learn to apply the teachings to your life right now!

Now don't get hung up on some of those strange names and places. Instead look for the principle, the point it's making. Then always ask the Lord to show you how to apply it to your life.

Using the above example, Proverbs 19:20, how can we apply it? By asking advice from godly people so we can make wise decisions . . . forever! Wisdom is something you keep a lifetime.

See how easy that was? The Bible is relevant for our lives today. Peter tells us it was written through men under the direction of the Holy Spirit (he told them what to write; see 2 Peter 1:21). The Holy Spirit guarded the truth to be sure it was accurate. Paul assures us that God's Word is indeed inspired by God himself. It is God-breathed!

Yes, it had to be translated into English. The Old Testament was originally written in Hebrew. The New Testament was written in Greek. Due to the painstaking process used by translators (under the watchful eye of the Holy Spirit) we can be confident that the words we read are authentic, accurate, reliable, and true.

Don't ever be fooled. The Word of God is more than a collection of stories and thoughts. It is spirit and life! God's Word is alive and active. By the power of the Holy Spirit, it speaks to us, teaches us, gives us direction, and it provides us with wisdom to make godly decisions.

God's Word is our up-to-the-minute map. It is the main way God will use to guide us over the mountains, across the rivers, and through the downpours of life. Do you want to know God's direction for your life? READ THE MAP!

REST STOP, EXIT HERE

1. Start today by reading 2 Timothy 3:16. This verse shows us four purposes for God's Word. Using a dictionary, define each of these key words:

Teaching—

_____

_____

_____

Reproof—

_____

_____

_____

Correction—

_____

_____

_____

(There's more!)

Training—

_____

_____

_____

Now, in your own words, rewrite this verse in a way that will help you remember it:

_____

_____

_____

_____

2. Explain the *goal* of God's Word, found in 2 Timothy 3:17.

_____

_____

_____

_____

DAY THREE
A True Treasure Map

Are you convinced by now that God's Word can get you headed on the right highway? Great! We promise you won't be disappointed, especially when you read the Word as if you're hunting for treasure.

Of course, every part of the Bible is vital to the Christian life. Yet for our purposes—to discover God's general will—we suggest you start studying in Proverbs and the letters, which are also called the epistles (Romans through Jude). There you will begin to uncover all sorts of instructions, guidelines, warnings, and promises. These will give you direction and insight when you're faced with a decision and you want God's wisdom.

When you get to the point of memorizing these instructions, the Holy Spirit will bring them to your mind when you need them. It's God's way of talking to you.

For today, let's do an experiment. We want you to experience firsthand how to look for God's general will. So we suggest you spend today's time doing some digging!

The Book of James is full of practical instructions to live by. Let's comb the Scriptures in chapter one to see what we can learn. Get a separate notebook where you can keep track of what you find as you go through the books of the Bible.

As you read, record the book, chapter, verse, and the instruction. We'll help you get started.

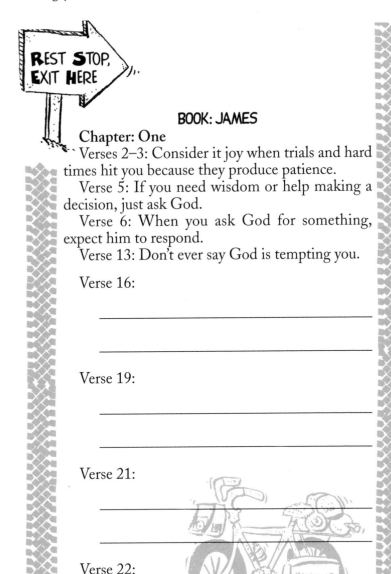

REST STOP, EXIT HERE

BOOK: JAMES

Chapter: One

Verses 2–3: Consider it joy when trials and hard times hit you because they produce patience.

Verse 5: If you need wisdom or help making a decision, just ask God.

Verse 6: When you ask God for something, expect him to respond.

Verse 13: Don't ever say God is tempting you.

Verse 16:

_____

_____

Verse 19:

_____

_____

Verse 21:

_____

_____

Verse 22:

_____

_____

Verse 25:

_____

_____

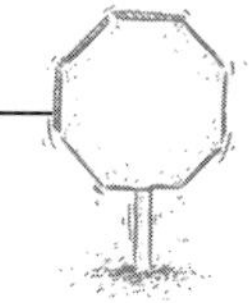

Verse 26:

_____

_____

Verse 27:

_____

_____

Wow! Look at all the instructions we found in just one chapter! What can we conclude about God's general will from these verses?

God desires for all of us to persevere when we go through hard things—don't jump ship, trust him. Perseverance or patience helps us develop strong character. He wants us to turn to him when we're stuck and need wisdom. He promises to pour it on us when we truly believe by faith that he'll answer us.

When you feel tempted, don't say it's God. He never tempts. It's Satan who does that. We are to be wise and not be deceived.

We also found out that not running our mouth and not being hot-tempered are part of God's best for us. We are also to be good listeners.

What about stuff like raunchy jokes, gossip, lies, dirty magazines, sexy novels, getting revenge? God says get rid of it. Instead, be glad for having heard the gospel and knowing the truth.

Next, don't just read the Bible, actually do what it says. Be obedient to God's instructions. Why? Because when you do it, you will be blessed!

Now a few more: God wants us to have control over our tongue, choose our words with love and wisdom, stay pure, and visit orphans and widows.

See how practical God's Word is? It really does show us God's general will for all believers. Now that you've started, challenge yourself to read one chapter of the Bible each day, looking for God's instructions.

If you get really energized, make a chart, listing God's instructions, truths, warnings, and promises. Or get some colored pencils. Assign a different color to each area. Simply underline each of them right in your Bible. Then, say you want to skim God's instructions, just look for the color that applies.

Try these:

Instructions—Green (for go)
Warnings—Red (for stop)
Truths—Blue (for honesty)
Promises—Yellow (for rays of hope)
Information about God, Jesus, the Holy
    Spirit—Purple (royalty)

DAY FOUR
Charting the Course

Andrea

A few months ago Bill and I escaped to the beach for some fun in the sun. We adore the sea gulls, the white sand, the hues of blues and greens in the water. In fact, I love it so much I decided to try to paint a beach scene using watercolors. I ended up painting the same scene five times, until I got it right. Over and over. It got tedious, but the more I painted, the more I understood what I needed to do to make it actually *look* like a beach scene!

Well, we truly want you to understand how very practical God's Word is so we're going to look up more Scriptures.

Second Timothy 3:16 says, "The whole Bible was given to us by inspiration from God and is useful to teach us what is true and to make us realize what is wrong in our lives; it straightens us out and helps us to do what is right."

Therefore, today we want you to pray and ask the Lord to help you see how he has mapped out his general will for your life. Then look up the following verses, recording how they teach you to live your life. These Scriptures apply to some hot, controversial teen topics!

Note: When you find an instruction or a Scripture that seems to apply to your situation, be sure to read the verses around it. Then check out the author of that book and to whom it was written. You need to be cautious about taking Scriptures out of context. Be sure they mean what they mean, not what you *want* them to mean!

37

REST STOP, EXIT HERE

GOD'S GENERAL WILL FOR MY LIFE

1. James 4:8

_____

_____

2. Colossians 3:20

_____

_____

3. Philippians 4:6

_____

_____

4. 1 Thessalonians 4:3–5

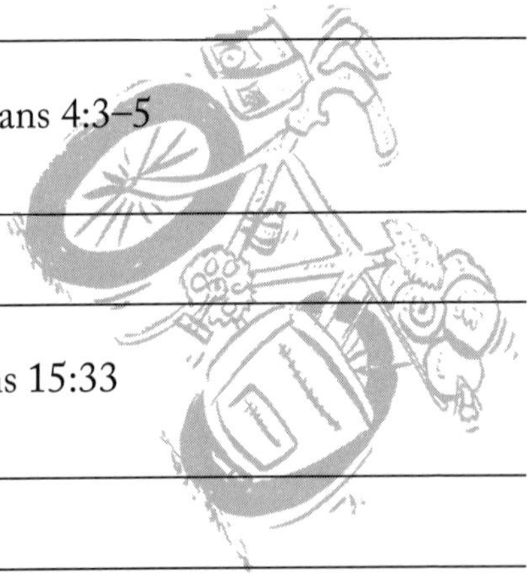

_____

_____

5. 1 Corinthians 15:33

_____

_____

6. Ephesians 4:32

_____

_____

7. Luke 6:31

_____

_____

8. 1 Peter 4:2–3

_____

_____

9. Ephesians 4:29

_____

_____

10. Matthew 5:43–44

_____

_____

DAY FIVE
Jesus: The Man to Imitate

Bill

One of my role models as I was contemplating God's call to be a pastor was Lyle Patterson of Wadena, Iowa. Lyle was a farmer in his late fifties who was also a leader in the small church where I was interning. Lyle was always loving and positive in all that he did. While I had doubts about my ability and future, Lyle believed in me. He listened to me and gave me honest Christian counsel. He invested his life in mine and made a difference in my life. In the late 1980s Lyle was killed in a farm accident. I flew from California back to Iowa for the funeral and noticed seven other interns at the funeral whose lives, like mine, had been touched by Lyle Patterson. Now I am trying to be a "Lyle Patterson" to two young men in our church who are contemplating ministry.

There is another role model, one that God gave to each of us. His name is Jesus. Since God wants us to be Christlike, Jesus is our example to follow. **The life of Jesus reveals (much of) God's will for our lives!** If we look intently at Jesus' personal life and the way he dealt with others, we will discover the way God wants us to live our lives.

So where do we find these discoveries? In the map, the Bible. (You knew we were going to say that, didn't you?) Jesus' journey here on earth was flawless. He always did God's will. In fact Jesus boldly exclaimed to the Jews who were trying to nail him for doing wrong, "I do not seek My own will, but the will of Him who sent Me" (John 5:30 NASB). Jesus only did what God directed him to do. Incredible.

Jesus tried to explain this same idea to his disciples. Apparently it had been a long day of traveling from Judea toward Galilee. They stopped for the night in Samaria. The disciples went into town for groceries while Jesus chatted with a woman at the well. When the disciples returned with a basket of fried chicken and mashed potatoes (okay, not really), Jesus wouldn't eat. It bugged them! "Rabbi, eat!" they said. But Jesus responded, "My food is to do the will of Him who sent Me, and to accomplish His work" (John 4:34 NASB). Imagine that. Doing what God asked, knowing he was fulfilling his Father's call, was the very thing that nourished Jesus. It was his heartbeat, his passion, his life. It fed him! It kept his spiritual tank full!

That's why we can confidently look to Jesus to see first-hand God's will for all his children. We can trust Jesus' example. He will teach us God's desire for our beliefs, our actions, and our reactions.

Take prayer, for instance. One thing Jesus did regularly was to retreat to a quiet place to talk to his Father (Matthew 14:23; Luke 6:12). Therefore, we know it is God's will for us to do the same.

One of Jesus' greatest qualities was the compassion he felt toward others. Compassion is similar to kindness, caring, sympathy, mercy, and tenderness. Jesus was able to see a person's need, to feel what he or she felt. But he didn't stop there. Jesus' compassion moved him to action! Read Matthew 14:14 and Matthew 15:32–37 to see what he did. God's will is for his children to be compassionate, kind, and caring like Jesus.

Of course, the greatest thing Jesus did was something only he could do. Only Jesus could have given his life as a sacrifice for our sin. Because of his willingness to be obedient to God's plan, we are able to be part of God's family. Though God may not ask us to give up our lives, we can imitate Jesus' selflessness and his great love for others.

REST STOP, EXIT HERE

The best way to see how Jesus shows us God's will is to read the Gospels and study his life! Just to get you started, read these verses and record how we can be like Jesus. Then when you find yourself in difficult situations, ask "What would Jesus do?"

Matthew 8:14: We can pray for others to be

_____.

John 13:34: We are to _____ one another.

Mark 2:5: We can _____ and not

hold grudges.

Luke 4:1–13: We can fight Satan by using

God's _____.

Matthew 11:1: We can _____ others

about the Kingdom of God.

John 5:30: We can be obedient to God's

_____.

Philippians 2:5–7: We can empty or humble

ourselves and be _____ to others.

Here's a basic Bible breakdown to give you an overview of this great book! There are two major segments:

1. **The Old Testament.** This includes 39 of the 66 books of the Bible and reveals God's arrangements with his people based on the Law.
2. **The New Testament.** This includes the other 27 books and reveals God's arrangement with his people based on Jesus' work on the cross.

Each major segment has four subsegments:

The Old Testament:

1. Genesis through Deuteronomy = God's Law
2. Joshua through Esther = Books of History
3. Job through Solomon = Books of Poetry
4. Isaiah through Malachi = Books of Prophecy

The New Testament:

1. Matthew through John = Gospels; the Life of Jesus
2. Acts = History of the Early Church
3. Romans through Jude = Letters containing doctrine, or how to live as a Christian
4. Revelation = End-time Prophecy

MERGING TRAFFIC

*Surrendering Your
Will to God*

DAY ONE
Me? Merge?

We pulled her little hand away six times! We told her no-no. Yet our niece, Katie Marie, continued to reach for that fragrant dish of potpourri. Was she purposely trying to test our patience? Probably not at age one and a half. But she *was* doing what comes naturally. She was exercising her will.

We are all born with a will. Will can be defined as one's mind-set, or a determination to do something, a desire to control one's own actions. We want to do what we want, when we want to do it! Most of us are naturally strong-willed, selfish people.

Then we meet Christ. The Holy Spirit comes to live inside us. Suddenly we have a choice. Will we continue to do it our own way or will we surrender our wills to God?

To surrender means to make a conscious choice to bring your will under the control of God's will. It means to yield your life to God's plan—rather than approaching life with your premade plans, goals, and dreams, you first go to God to seek his plans, goals, and dreams for you!

Many Christians foolishly say no to Jesus at this point. Oh, sure, they want God to give them eternal life, forgiveness of sins, and comfort when they're sad. But watch them dig in their heels when it comes to their plans! They want control. Too bad, too. The wisest thing we will ever do after receiving Christ is to put our hands in his. There is joy and peace in following his will.

When you yield your will, God can really begin to do a good work in you and through you. Philippians 2:13 (NASB) tells us that "it is God who is at work in you, both to will and to work for His good pleasure." That's how it works. He gives you the will, the desire to be in his will. Then he shows you the how-to! He guides, then provides!

If you are struggling in some area to discover what God wants you to do, check to see how yielded you truly are. Are you willing to do what he shows you? He has laid out his general plan in his Word, but chances are he won't show you the specific directions of his plan for you until you are yielded.

Yielding, surrendering, and merging your will with God's does not mean you lose. It doesn't mean you give in. Surrendering to God is not like being on the battlefield and raising your little white flag in defeat. God is not our enemy who is trying to beat us down until we give up!

> *Get your orders from Headquarters!*

When we surrender to God, WE WIN! How's that? Because there is no better place to be than in GOD'S WILL. We guarantee it!

46

1. Paul was a highly educated man, a respected Pharisee and teacher of the Law who spoke against the claims of Christ. He arrested and put to death many Christians. Then Jesus got ahold of him! Find out what Paul has to say about his life after yielding it to Jesus. Read Philippians 3:4–8 and 1 Timothy 1:12–17.

2. Because Paul had seen God work in his own life, he was able to share this message with others. Look up Philippians 1:6. How does it make you feel to know that God won't give up on you?

   _____

   _____

3. If you give your life fully to Christ, will it be a boring drudge? Check it out in Psalm 37:4. List three ways you could delight yourself in the Lord. Start today!

   _____

   _____

   _____

DAY TWO
Letting God Drive

Bill

I grew up in Iowa, where the winters are cold, snowy, and long. There were days of fierce winds with temperatures near zero. But that didn't stop me from running. It just meant more clothes! First a knit cap, next my hood, and then a scarf tied around my neck and over my mouth. Totally covered, I was ready. A chilly run would energize my body, training my muscles and increasing my endurance!

Running, one of the many sports I enjoyed, was a major focus in my life as a high schooler. I broke six school records. When I was offered a track scholarship at a nearby college, I was pumped. College track proved just as exciting and gratifying as high school. I lettered as a freshman. As a sophomore I broke two school records in the triple jump and mile relay.

Then the strangest thing happened. Within a short period of time, I injured my left ankle three times. The first injury happened when I accidentally stepped on a soda can, the second when I was shooting hoops with some guys from the dorm. The third time, I was walking across a field on my way home from track practice when I stepped in a hole.

After the third time, as I iced the ankle, feeling irritated that I would be watching the next track meet from the sidelines, I wondered if God was trying to get my attention.

Indeed he was! He used my ankle injuries to slow me down so I could rethink my life. I had accepted Christ when I was in eighth grade. I knew he had called me to be a minister. Yet, my focus was still sports.

47

I bowed my head and committed my entire life to Christ, asking him to direct me.

In a short time, he opened the way for me to transfer to a Christian college, becoming a Bible major. After graduation, I went on to seminary.

In each of our lives there comes a time when we allow Jesus to become the driver. We slide over, content to be his passenger. I've learned this is the best way to go. Jesus is not only the best driver possible, he knows the map better than any of us.

Allow Jesus to be the driver in your life. And be sure to buckle up. It will be exciting to see in which direction he will steer your life!

1. David Livingstone is our favorite medical missionary. In our workout room at home, we have these words of his hanging on our wall:

> Lord, send me anywhere,
>   Only go with me.
> Lay any burden on me,
>   Only sustain me.
> Sever any tie but the tie
>   That binds me to Thyself.

Take a few moments to ponder his words. What do they mean to you?

_____

_____

2. There was a very wealthy young man, sort of a yuppie type, who lived in Jesus' day. He was a good person who kept the Ten Commandments. But when Jesus challenged him to let go of his will and follow Christ, what happened? See Matthew 19:16–22.

_____

_____

DAY THREE
Changing Paths!

Andrea

Lights. Camera. ACTION! When I was a teen, this was my goal. More than anything, I wanted my face on magazine covers. I wanted to be the star of the runway, dazzling audiences with the latest fashions. I practiced turns and poses in front of the bathroom mirror, dreaming of the day I would be a real model.

That day came for me when I signed a contract with Wilhelmina Models in New York City. I was nineteen.

The first year was fun and exciting. I worked with lots of photographers and had some exciting jobs. I appeared on several magazine covers, fashion catalogs, and commercials.

Besides the modeling, New York was a blast to me: so many types of people, the coolest shopping, great restaurants. My favorite was Tavern on the Green. It twinkled at night with atmosphere, right there in Central Park.

And speaking of the park, it was always alive. Sunday afternoons were the best. Joggers, skaters, people on picnics, horse-and-buggy rides. There were always musicians, mimes, jugglers, and magicians performing for laughs and tips.

I was also thrilled every time I met someone "famous"— Tony Danza, Sylvester Stallone, Billy Dee Williams, Reggie Jackson, Mia Farrow, Sela Ward. What fun!

Well, at least for a while.

I had accepted Christ earlier in life but never really developed a relationship with him. So I had plowed ahead with my plans for the future. I told God what I wanted and expected him to bless it!

Little by little, my plans started to crumble. I wasn't happy trying to make it as a model. Deep inside I felt a tug from the Holy Spirit. Did God want something else for me? Through a series of events, the Lord showed me I was making the wrong choices. I was on the wrong pathway. I knew deep in my heart that I had pursued my life without seeking God's direction. Now it was time to give myself to him 100 percent. I wanted to be on his pathway for me.

It was hard for me to leave New York. I was closing the door on my dream. I had to let it go. But I trusted that God himself, who loved me more than I could even imagine, would lead me to something even better.

> *Your desire to please God has to override your desire to please yourself!*

As I watched for his leading in my life, he was, and still is, faithful to show me the way. Proverbs 3:6 says, "In everything you do, put God first, and he will direct you and crown your efforts with success."

Saying yes to God's plan is not a one-time deal. Every day we must choose because we will always be faced with the temptation to go it alone and leave God behind.

DON'T DO IT! Make it your life's goal to say yes to God's will every single day. Put him first in all you do and he will direct you—just like he did me.

Can I honestly say that walking in tune with Christ is better than being out of his will, out modeling in New York? You betcha! Obeying the Lord has brought me clear direction, inner joy, and a calming peace that only *he* can give. Lights? Camera? Action? No, thanks. I'll take Jesus.

REST STOP, EXIT HERE

1. John the Baptist knew God had called him for a special purpose. He knew his role in life. In John 3:30 (NASB) he wisely states, "He [meaning Jesus] must increase, but I must decrease." Pray, asking the Lord to show you areas in your life where you are not putting him first. How can you decrease and allow God to increase in your life?

_____

_____

_____

_____

2. Drop it all for Christ? Check out Matthew 4:18–22. What kind of changes do you think Peter, Andrew, James, and John had to make as they adjusted their lives to Jesus' plan for them? What might they have felt? What would you have done?

_____

_____

_____

_____

Success:
Success:
Success:
Success:

Finding Out What God Wants You to Do and Doing It!

DAY FOUR
The Ultimate Surrender

The sun was setting far beyond the olive trees that filled the garden of Gethsemane. The shadows from the branches were fading as the dusk turned into night. He had separated himself from the others. The reality of his mission was pressing in on him. Jesus fell on his face in agony and despair.

Tears and sweat dripped from his body. His soul was "crushed with horror and sadness to the point of death." With his head in his hands, he prayed, using the bit of breath he could force out. "My Father! If it is possible, let this cup be taken away from me. But I want your will, not mine" (Matthew 26:38–39).

What? Jesus wanted to pass on this plan? He didn't want this cup? The cup represented what he was about to do. It stood for the sins of man, which were sending him to the cross. It stood for the cruel treatment and horrifying death he was about to experience. Who wanted to be spit on, beaten, and nailed to a cross, left for dead? Besides, he knew he would be temporarily cut off from God, his loving Father. I'll bet he was thinking, *Father, I don't know if I can do this!*

It was all too much for his human side. Part of him didn't want to face the cross. He was scared. He was human, just like us. But he was also divine. He knew he was the only one who could answer this call. This was the Father's plan for him. He had a choice. He submitted. He surrendered his will. Jesus wanted to please his Father; he wanted the Father's will, not his own.

What about you?

54

After you've told God how *you* want it to be, are you willing to say, "*but*, Father, I want for me what you want for me"? God's will over yours—this is tough stuff. Not for weenies! Allowing God to set the course and call the shots takes commitment. Are you sold out to God?

When you're seeking God's will, you must be willing to pray, like Jesus, "Lord, your will be done, not mine" instead of "my will be done, not yours."

Jesus' flesh—his human nature—wanted to say, "No way. I'm outta here." But by the power of the Holy Spirit within him, he said yes. He went to the cross.

How can we say yes, as well? By remembering who lives in us! The Holy Spirit! When your flesh is weak and wants to say no, rely on the Spirit to give you the strength to say yes. Then when you turn, taking steps toward God's plan, the power will be there. God will enable you to follow through.

God's will is always best. It may be harder but it brings greater reward. Surrendering your will brings a heart full of peace, contentment, and deep joy, knowing you are doing the right thing, knowing you have said, "Thy will be done."

Surrender: Joyfully Placing Your Hand in the Trustworthy Palm of the Lord, Allowing Him to Lead

1. Do you think it is important to God that you do his will? Read these verses and decide for yourself! Mark 3:31–35; Matthew 7:21; John 15:5–10; Matthew 6:9–10; 1 John 2:17.

_____

_____

2. Your goal in life can be the same goal Jesus had in his life. Discover this goal in John 5:30 and John 4:34. Now read 1 Peter 4:2. How are you to live out your time here on earth?

_____

_____

_____

3. You are a part of God's overall plan here on earth. God uses people to get his will accomplished. Therefore, there is something special he wants you to do. What if you say no? What if Jesus refused the cross or Noah refused to build the ark? Suppose Paul wouldn't preach the gospel to the Gentiles? What if the disciples had kept Jesus a secret? You will never know how God planned to use you if you say no. Pray now, committing yourself to his will for your life.

DAY FIVE
Divided Highway

Brad took one last puff off the cigarette, then flicked the butt out the window. The fan had chased away the last of the smoke, so he turned it off. He was glad his room was on the second floor. He felt confident those butts always landed in the wooded lot next door.

The phone rang. It was Glenn, calling to remind him of the meeting place. Tonight would be like no other. Not only did they have a case of beer, but Glenn's older brother had gotten some cocaine. Expensive, but he was eager to try it.

Brad closed his bedroom door and headed down the stairs. He could hear the laughter of his brother and his friends coming from the family room. They had just returned from a Fellowship of Christian Athletes competition night.

"Hey, Brad, we missed you at the meeting," his brother's friend Sam called out. "Want to join us for a pizza?"

"Can't tonight," Brad replied reluctantly.

"Okay, man. Catch you tomorrow at Sunday school." Sam smiled and waved.

The warmth of the summer air hit Brad's face as he headed toward his car, but it didn't begin to warm up the chill that hit his heart.

What am I doing? I'm such a liar. I can barely stand myself.

The fight was starting again in the arena of his mind.

God, I want to live like a Christian and do the stuff I know pleases you, but then again I don't. I want to party and do whatever I want.

The pressure in Brad's chest was almost too much as he turned the corner, heading to the meeting place.

Brad has a problem. It's called being double-minded. It's a battle of wills. He wants to be able to party all weekend, then sit in church on Sunday feeling holy. It doesn't work. A person can't be on two roads at the same time. It's like trying to blend oil and water. You can shake them up till your arm is about to fall off, but when you stop, they will separate again. They just don't mix!

When Christians try to live like Brad, they don't have any peace in their lives. There's always a tug from one side or the other. You see, when Christ lives in you, he brings a new set of values and standards to live by. When you choose to do things according to the world's standards, you are in direct opposition to *yourself.*

Being a Christian and living in an ungodly way creates inner conflict. One foot in the kingdom of God and one foot in the world doesn't work. They don't mix. You can't blend them. It's like riding the fence; you'll get splinters!

So, what to do? Swing both feet over the fence and plant both in God's kingdom. You will only have peace in your life when you are on *one* road—God's!

1. Jonah was a man who sought after his will, not God's. The Lord even showed him specifically what he wanted him to do, but Jonah refused. The result? Jonah had no peace. Read Jonah 1:1–4, 15–17. When Jonah surrendered his will, peace followed. See Isaiah 48:18. When you follow God's standards, what do you receive?

_____

_____

_____

_____

2. Read James 1:6–8. What can unstable, double-minded people expect from God? How does God want us to seek him and live the Christian life—half-heartedly or whole-heartedly? Find out in Jeremiah 29:11–13 and 1 Chronicles 28:9.

_____

_____

_____

(There's more!)

3. God wants us to put him first. Read Matthew
   6:33. What happened to Lot's wife when she
   looked back at what she was leaving behind
   (see Genesis 19:26)? Is God in first or second
   place in your life?

   _____

   _____

   _____

   _____

   _____

4. Read Romans 8:5–8. Is your life set on the
   flesh or the Spirit? Pray, asking the Lord to
   help you get both feet on his road, pursuing
   the things of the Spirit.

   _____

   _____

   _____

   _____

   _____

   _____

It's been said that:

> Your life is a gift
> *from* God.
> What you do with it
> is your gift
> *to* God!

Here are some things God has done for us. They are perfect reasons to say "yes" to his will!

- He loves us (1 John 4:9–10)
- He paid the penalty for our sins through Jesus (Colossians 2:13–14)
- He offers us eternal life with him in heaven (John 3:16)
- He comforts us in our sorrows (2 Corinthians 1:3–5)
- He provides encouragement and perseverance (Romans 15:5)
- He protects us (Psalm 91:11)
- He hears our prayers (1 John 5:14–15)

Will you exchange your will for his?

GOTTA-HAVE-IT GEAR

Traveling Tools for the Journey

DAY ONE
Bring Out the Binoculars!

You're studying the map. You're beginning to see the general direction of your life. But you can't seem to find the specifics—the roads, bridges, or interstates with *your* name on them, the exact directions for you.

Is it true that God has a specific will for each of our lives? The Bible seems to indicate that he does.

> You saw me before I was born and scheduled each day of my life before I began to breathe. Every day was recorded in your Book!
>
> Psalm 139:16

> The Lord will work out his plans for my life—for your lovingkindness, Lord, continues forever. Don't abandon me—for you made me.
>
> Psalm 138:8

Bring out the binoculars and look again!

Since we know God's Word is true, we can pinpoint the *facts* in these verses. Fact one: the Lord made us; he saw us while we were being formed! Fact two: he has scheduled each day of our lives. Fact three: he will work out his plans for our lives!

Great! God knows the plan. His part is to work it out in our lives. Fabulous. Awesome. Excellent. So why do we often feel lost in a cloud of confusion, a tunnel of turmoil?

We have to do our part, too. We have to seek him, put him in the center of our lives and maintain a loving relationship with him. Discovering God's specific will for our lives is the result of consistent communion with him. When we are constantly talking to God, we will be close enough to recognize his voice, to feel his leading. Then we must trust and obey what he shows us.

HINT: Don't let the guidance become more important than God. Seek him and guidance follows!

God will reveal the specifics for our lives that are absolutely necessary. For example, he may impress on you to go to a Christian college, but he may not tell you exactly which one.

God will be faithful to work out his plan in your life. It will require patience and trust on your part. Why? Because he doesn't share the whole plan with you all at once. He leads one step at a time. Psalm 119:105 confirms this; it says that God's Word is a lamp to our feet and a light to our path. The Lord lights the pathway right at our feet so we can see where to take the next step! One step at a time. He doesn't shine a headlight down the road so we can see who we'll marry, what career we'll have, or where we'll live. He shows us one step at a time. Therefore we would be wise to walk with him daily, stay tight, so we'll know the specifics of his plan.

The specifics of God's plan will always line up with the general plan he lays out in his Word. God will NEVER tell you to do something that contradicts his Word.

There is no formula to discovering God's specific plan, just a relationship that is close enough for you to see his hand working out the details of your life. However, there are a few tools that will help you recognize God's leading. When each of these tools line up or come together, you can trust God is revealing his plan. You'll discover these traveling tools this week.

God was very specific when he laid out his plan for Noah. He didn't just say, "Hey, Noah, go build a boat and load it up with all sorts of stuff 'cause there's going to be a major rainstorm." Read Genesis 6:9–22 and answer the following.

Why did God choose Noah (v. 9)?

_____

What was the ark to be made of (v. 14)?

_____

How long was the ark to be (v. 15)?

_____

How wide was it to be (v. 15)?

_____

How high was it to be (v. 15)? (A cubit is thought to have been 18 inches, making the ark 450 feet long, 75 feet wide, and 45 feet high.)

_____

(There's more!)

Was the ark to have windows (v. 16)?

_____

How many decks (v. 16)?

_____

What was Noah to take with him (vv. 19–21)?

_____

_____

_____

God does not change! If he was specific with Noah, he'll be specific with you when he needs to be. Just do what Noah did—WALK WITH GOD!

DAY TWO
Catch That Cool Canteen!

It's hot. You've been traveling for days. The road is dusty; the air is dismal. Up ahead there is no sight of town. Your feet are blistered, your muscles weary from travel. "Am I sure this is the way?" you ask yourself, unable to concentrate or focus.

Ah, a tree. Shade. A chance to rest. You feel the bit of breeze. A few pockets of cooler air caress your face.

A long drink of water from your canteen floods away your thirst. Refreshing. Little by little you're feeling better, revived with new strength to help you continue the journey.

Wouldn't it be great if there really were an oasis like that, where you could get revived, refreshed, and refocused on life's journey, a place to double-check the map to be sure you haven't wandered off onto the wrong road?

Well, there is! It's called the Secret Place. It's where you come apart from the world to be alone with the Lord to read his Word and to talk to him in prayer. The Secret Place is where you put yourself in the frame of mind to hear from God. The Bible says that "he that dwelleth in the secret place of the most High shall abide under the shadow of the Almighty" (Psalm 91:1 KJV).

There are some *key* words in this verse. "Dwell" is one of them. To dwell means to stay in a certain place. To dwell in the Secret Place means to go there often—physically *and* in your mind. It's a special place where you can talk to the Lord.

Another key word is "abide." Abide is similar to dwell, but in a stronger sense. To abide somewhere means to live

67

there, to belong there. Where? Under the shadow of the Almighty. These key words mean to continually be under the protective arm of the Lord, under his care and guidance. In the Secret Place you can experience God's comfort, encouragement, forgiveness, unending love, and DIRECTION.

Can you imagine knowing there is such a wonderful place but rarely going there? Many travelers long to be there, to develop that intimate, one-on-one relationship with their Creator, but they're too busy. Oh, they intend to stop off for a while, but intentions don't get them anywhere.

So they try to keep traveling in their own strength, struggling to find their way. They turn to other things to sustain them or help them escape. Eventually they're too tired to care.

Though they blame God, they are at fault. God can't make us stop off at his Secret Place. It's up to us. The more we visit the more we will want to dwell there, but it takes a sacrifice of time, a commitment from the heart.

Having a Secret Place, a quiet time with Jesus is vital to hearing him speak to you. In fact, the key to hearing God's voice is taking time to be alone with him in his word. The Scripture says to be still and know that he is God (Psalm 46:10). It's your choice. Are you willing to set aside the time to be in his presence, to pray, to ask for his wisdom, to listen for his voice? Don't cheat yourself! Make the time to come into the Lord's presence. Dwell in the Secret Place.

1. Your Secret Place needs to be a quiet place where you can focus on what you are reading and praying for. Read Matthew 6:6. Jesus suggests an "inner room" where the door is closed. In other words, no TV, no radio, no screaming sisters! This could be in the house or out in the backyard under a tree. Where could your Secret Place be?

_____

_____

_____

_____

2. Read Psalm 5:1–3. Though any time is a good time to be with the Lord, why do you think talking with God at the start of your day is better? What would be the value of praying over your day's activities, tests, sports practice, etc.?

_____

_____

_____

_____

DAY THREE
The Compass

Bill

Karl breezed into youth group one night all excited. "It was like really cool, dude. I was just jammin' down the pavement eating a raisin bagel, totally minding my own stuff, when this bird like came flyin' out of just nowhere and it did a dive bomb, right at me, man. It made a straight beeline directly toward me, then a twist to the left and up into the sky it sailed. Hey, that's when I knew. It hit me: God must be telling me I'm supposed to be a fighter pilot!"

A sign from God? Sounds more like a hungry pigeon trying to get a little breakfast bagel!

Circumstances—the events that occur in a situation—can be a part of the way God chooses to give you direction. They can work like a compass. But beware. Every little thing that happens is not a hand-delivered sign from God. So when can circumstances be trusted? Only after you have studied to see what God's Word says about your situation. Then, when you have surrounded your problem or need for God's direction in prayer, remember that the main way the Holy Spirit guides is through his Word. Then he will often impress a direction on us when we are one-on-one with him in prayer, asking his wisdom. Always ask God to give you his perspective on your circumstances.

Circumstances are most likely to be a part of God's direction when they *confirm* or back up the direction in which you already feel God is leading you.

70

I mentioned earlier how, as a sophomore at the University of Northern Iowa, I thought God was trying to get my attention with a series of ankle injuries. As I spent time in prayer, I rededicated my life to Christ. I told the Lord that if he wanted me to change colleges I would.

Several weeks later I was home visiting my family when a friend of my dad's came over. He brought me an information packet on a Christian college. Right away I knew that this was from God. I felt assured that I was to leave the state college and go to the Christian college.

The circumstances confirmed what I already sensed to be the direction God was leading. It turned out to be God's answer to my prayer. Oftentimes God will use circumstances to confirm his plan for you.

If you have read the Word and have prayed (not just once or twice, either) and you still don't have a clue, then ask the Lord to show you what to do. Watch to see how he might be working around you. Just don't get sucked into trying to read every event or interpret every change as God's heavenly hint!

Always go back to him to seek his guidance, asking if the circumstances are an open door or a closed door. God truly does want you to know his answers to your prayers. He wants you to hear his call in a certain direction. He wants you to come away to hide under the shadow of his protective wing to seek his answers for you!

72

1. Circumstances can be tricky. It might seem like you are in the worst situation possible, but nevertheless, God is still in control! Read Mark 4:35–41. What were the circumstances of the disciples? How did they feel? Who was ultimately in control of those circumstances? What things in your life seem out of control? Pray, asking God to help you remember that he is still in charge!

_____

_____

2. The Bible will always give us God's perspective on a circumstance. Let's say you've asked God to help you pass your history exam. Right before class, the guy in front of you is passing around cheat sheets with the right answers— he stole them off the teacher's desk. Could this be God's way of helping you? Check it out against the Bible. Read Psalm 51:6. What does it say about breaking rules in 2 Timothy 2:5? Was the cheat sheet God's answer?

_____

_____

DAY FOUR
Walkie-Talkie: The Way to Call for Help!

Andrea

Life was so confusing! I had just left my modeling career in New York. I moved back to Tulsa where my family lived. I knew the Lord had told me to do this, but I was clueless as to what should come next. Should I do nothing? Live at home? Get an apartment? Get a job? Go to college? Find a husband? Leave for the mission field? I didn't know what God wanted! Or what I wanted (except that I wanted to do what God wanted—WHATEVER THAT WAS).

I didn't seem to be able to sort through the rubble on my own, so I consulted a special Christian friend of mine. She had been walking with the Lord longer than I had, she knew the Bible, and she was older and more mature than I was. Her godly wisdom helped me see that getting a job would help me get a productive start. Then I would have the money to get a car so I could even drive myself to school. Several months later, when it was time to enroll in school, God opened a way for me to use some scholarship money I had earned several years earlier in pageants to pay for tuition!

The Lord used that mature Christian woman to guide me. He will often use other Christians to speak to us. Their godly advice can help us see God's plan. These special people are often called "mentors," a word that means a trusted counselor.

Proverbs 11:14 (NASB) says, "Where there is no guidance, the people fall, But in abundance of counselors there is victory." If you have no guidance you will flounder and be easy prey for Satan, so seek the counsel of a godly person you can trust, someone who will cheer you on and coach you in the game of life. This should be a person who can help you sort through the Bible, your prayer impressions, circumstances, and emotions so you can discern God's guidance in every situation.

Pray and ask the Lord to show you who could be a mentor to you. Guys should choose a man, and girls should choose a woman—perhaps your parents, pastor, youth director, coach, teacher, an aunt or uncle, Campus Life or Young Life leader, or a mature Christian from your church. Use this list as a guideline. Keep your spiritual eyes open! God will show you the right person!

Mentor Match-Ups
- A person who is committed to the Lord
- A person who loves and cares for you
- A person who is older in years and mature in his or her faith
- A person who will pray with you
- A person from whom you can receive discipline or correction
- A person who you trust will have your best interest at heart
- A person who will be honest and tell you the truth (even if it's not what you want to hear)
- A person who knows you well, who can help you see your natural talents and gifts from God

1. We need our brothers and sisters in Christ. God designed us to be a *body;* we were not meant to make it alone. Check out these other verses about godly counsel: Proverbs 1:7; Proverbs 13:10; Proverbs 19:20; and Psalm 1:1.

2. Though a mentor needs to be someone older than you, it is a surge of support to have Christian friends. Choose friends who are on the same road you are on, who will influence you for good, who will pray for you and be a support! Of course, to find that kind of friend, you have to *be* that kind of friend. Read about Jonathan and David's supportive friendship in 1 Samuel 18:1–4 and 1 Samuel 20.

3. God can use godly people in another way—through something they say. Maybe something your pastor or Sunday school teacher or someone else says catches your attention and applies to the situation you've been praying about. The person may have no idea he or she said something that helped you, yet God can use it to give you guidance.

DAY FIVE
Paving the Road with Peace

Bill

One of my favorite things in the whole world is to go to Wrigley Field in Chicago to watch the Cubs play baseball. I like to arrive at least an hour before game time to watch the players take batting practice.

The position players run and stretch and the pitchers warm up their arms. The lineups are announced and the national anthem is sung. Then the two coaches meet with the four umpires at home plate to go over the rules. The umpires play an important role in each game. It is their job to keep order and to determine right from wrong. Without the umpires there would be chaos and baseball wouldn't be the great game it is.

The umpire calls the shots of the game. He's the guy who makes the final decisions. There is an umpire in the Bible, too. His name is Peace. Colossians 3:15 (AMP) says to let peace be the umpire in our lives, to let peace be the ruler of our hearts.

Peace is a quiet, inner confidence, a calmness. God's peace is not affected by the craziness going on around you. He doesn't promise outer peace, but inner peace. He often uses this inner peace as a confirmation that you have discovered his direction. It's the Holy Spirit's way of saying, "This is it, baby! Go for it!"

When you're rattling the gates of heaven, trying to get God's answer for direction, peace is probably not going to immediately pour down on you. First you need to study God's Word; then ask him for wisdom. Next, check out the circumstances and talk to your "mentor." Finally, pray and ask the Lord to fill your heart with his peace so you will know exactly what he wants you to do.

Instant peace may not be your instant answer. If you just pick any old direction, instant peace may really just be a huge sense of relief that you finally made a decision! Give it a few days, a week, maybe longer.

Prolonged peace is the key to being sure of God's direction or answer.

What if you have no peace? Then don't do anything until you go back and seek the Lord again!

And if you only feel a tiny bit of peace toward one direction? Then ask the Lord to flood you with peace as you take a step in that direction. Often a full sense of peace arrives as you move to action. However, if you get started and realize you've now lost the little bit of peace you had, back off. Back to prayer you go. Wait for the umpire to make the call!

As You Listen for God's Will, You Can Trust That You'll Hear Him.

How?

He is the Good Shepherd.
John 10:11

You are his sheep.
Psalm 100:3

His sheep hear his voice.
John 10:27

He has given you his Word on it!

1. Is it true God leads through peace? Read Isaiah 55:12. Pray and let peace help you make your decision. Close your eyes. Take a deep breath. Which option seems to promise the most peace *from God?* Go with it!

2. God wants you to live in his peace. Sounds great, but how? By giving him all your worries, fears, big decisions. Read Philippians 4:6–7. What things do you need to give to God so he can flood your heart and mind with peace?

_____

_____

_____

_____

_____

_____

_____

_____

What's in Your Backpack?

Pull it off your shoulders, set it down, and undo the front clasp. Now take a peek inside. Look deeper. What's in your back-pack? What attitudes are you carrying around with you on your journey through life?

As you yield your life to the Holy Spirit, there are some attitudes that will become evident. They are the fruit or results of God's Spirit in you. Though it is his job to produce these attitudes, you can certainly hinder his prog-ress. You can choose to work with the Holy Spirit or to dig in your heels and refuse.

Here are the attitudes God wants you to have filling your backpack and shining through your life.

Attitude of Love

To unconditionally love others, even if they have been unloving to you. Not being selfish and rude.

Attitude of Joy

To show joy, even when life is crumbling around you, trusting God is in control. Not being depressed or grumpy.

Attitude of Peace

To be worry free and content, even if you don't have all the answers. Not being totally stressed out.

Attitude of Patience

To remain calm and be willing to wait even where there is pressure. Not demanding instant action.

Attitude of Kindness

To be tenderhearted, showing mercy and forgiveness toward others, even if they have mistreated you. Not being mean and revengeful.

Attitude of Goodness

To practice moral values even when others say, "If it feels good, do it." Not being deceitful.

Attitude of Faithfulness

To follow through and not grow weary in your well-doing, even when you are tempted to quit. Not giving in and giving up.

Attitude of Meekness

To show humility and boast in the Lord, not ourselves. Not being cocky and self-reliant.

Attitude of Self-Control

To show inward strength, restraining from doing or saying things that would not please the Lord. Not being ruled by temptations.

Take these positive attitudes with you as you journey through life with Jesus!

CROSSROADS

Rules for Remaining on the Right Road

DAY ONE
Obey the Law!

Josh steamed with anger. He had had it with his dad. He didn't care anymore. Saturday was his day off from school. He was sick of having to do everything his bossy dad told him to do. Who did he think he was, anyway, a slave boy? Scrub down the truck, sweep out the garage, collect the trash from the wastebaskets in every single room in the house, then dump them in the smelly old garbage cans outside. Josh hit his limit. No one was going to tell *him* what to do. He was not going to obey.

Mention the word obedience to most teens and you'll feel a wall of steel shoot up. The idea of doing what someone else tells you to do revs up most kids' rebellious rays. Obedience seems totally taboo in our society that preaches, "Live for yourself," "Look out for #1," "Do it your way."

Why do teens like Josh hate the word obedience? Maybe they don't really know what it means. Obedience is not being a slave. Obedience means to adjust yourself to the desires of another person, to choose to do what they want, not because you have to but because you want to. Obedience is a sign of love and respect.

Obedience proves you love the person you are obeying. What you *do* shows what you *believe*. Your actions confirm your inner convictions. Obedience is an outward expression of the inner love and respect you have for your parents, teachers, and others.

If Josh is wrestling so strongly against doing what his dad requests, imagine what will happen when *God* asks him to do something! His actions will let you know exactly where he stands with God.

Jesus said, "I will only reveal myself to those who love me and obey me. . . . Anyone who doesn't obey me doesn't love me" (John 14:23–24).

Gosh. Strong words from Jesus himself! If we love God, we'll obey. So, if we have a huge hang-up about obeying God, it means we have a huge hang-up about truly loving God.

When you deeply love the Lord, you will want to do what he asks. You will want to surrender your will to his. You will want to follow his lead. You will not only want him to give you direction in your life, you'll want to do it!

When God reveals his will to us, that's our key to start our engines, line up, and get moving! He doesn't show us his plan so we can *think* about it. He doesn't expect us to examine it, discuss it, debate it, consider it. He expects us to DO IT!

"And remember, it is a message to obey, not just to listen to. So don't fool yourselves. For if a person just listens and doesn't obey, he is like a man looking at his face in a mirror; as soon as he walks away, he can't see himself anymore or remember what he looks like. But if anyone keeps looking steadily into God's law for free men, he will not only remember it but he will do what it says, and God will greatly bless him in everything he does" (James 1:22–24).

Obedience is not drudgery; it's a blessing! Only when we follow the way God is leading will we see him work in our lives. When we see him at work, we know he's there! It makes our faith stronger. It makes our love deeper. It makes us want to be quick to obey.

1. Obedience does indeed bring blessings. Read Jeremiah 7:23–24. What happened when the people of Israel obeyed? What happened when they didn't obey? What other ways might obedience bring joy and blessing to our lives?

_____

_____

_____

2. James makes it clear that we are to *do* God's Word, not just hear it! Read James 1:22–25 and James 2:17. Doing God's Word proves what? Write a prayer asking the Lord to help you obey so as to prove your faith is alive!

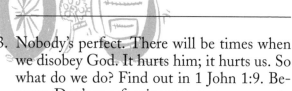

_____

_____

_____

3. Nobody's perfect. There will be times when we disobey God. It hurts him; it hurts us. So what do we do? Find out in 1 John 1:9. Beware: Don't use forgiveness as an excuse to disobey! Make obedience your goal!

DAY TWO
Memorize the Map!

Andrea

New York was months behind me. I was enrolled in Bible school, making strides at straightening out my life. New goals, new values, new friends.

During that time I attended the wedding reception of a friend. The guest list hadn't crossed my mind. But there they were. A couple of cool-as-ice babes from toyland. I could feel their stares as they downed their beers, "partying hearty." It was obvious I had changed. They saw it as their chance to ridicule me, cut me down to size.

When the whispers and laughs got to me, I darted to the women's restroom. Latching the door to the stall, I pressed my forehead against the cold enamel.

"Lord, I can't take this!" I cried.

Suddenly the words to a Scripture passage we had studied that week at school came to mind.

"But even if you should suffer for the sake of righteousness, you are blessed. And do not fear their intimidation, and do not be troubled" (1 Peter 3:14 NASB). Those words gave me the strength I needed to face the situation. I felt assured that the Lord was there by my side. That's the value of memorizing God's Word. It helps to keep you on the right road. I could have gotten ticked and told them off. Or I could have given in and drunk with them just so they'd accept me again. Instead, God's Word gave me the direction I needed.

When we memorize God's Word it's like inputting it into our brain's computer. We store it in our memory banks so the Holy Spirit can pull it out. When you are praying for a person or about a decision or when you find yourself in a predicament like I did, a verse of Scripture comes to your mind. That's the Holy Spirit using the Word of God to speak to you!

Perhaps he's giving you guidance, assurance, or comfort. Perhaps he's reminding you of the right thing to do so you won't sin!

> I have hidden your word in my heart
> that I might not sin against you.
> Psalm 119:11 NIV

His Word, memorized in our minds and hidden in our hearts, keeps us on the right road.

REST STOP, EXIT HERE

1. James 1:21 refers to the Word as being "implanted" in us! God's Word is to be deep in our hearts and minds; then it can spring up when we need it. Read Mark 4:1–20. Which soil are you? The road, the rocks, the thorns, or the good soil? How deep is God's Word planted in your memory?

_____

_____

2. Meditating on God's Word helps us to store it in our memory. To meditate means to continuously think deeply about something, to mull it over in your mind and heart. Read Psalm 1:1–3. What are some benefits of meditating on God's Word or Law?

_____

_____

3. Just like you can't retrieve a file you haven't saved, the Holy Spirit can't help you recall Scripture that's not in your brain! Say a prayer of commitment today to begin memorizing God's Word.

DAY THREE
Avoid Side Roads!

Andrea

Anna had managed to squeeze in a few meaningful moments of prayer before heading off to school. While her head was bowed, her friend Kari came to mind. Anna sensed the Lord was telling her to call and invite Kari to come over Friday night. Anna knew Kari's parents were in the middle of a divorce. All the fighting had left Kari feeling angry, frustrated, and sad, all mixed together.

Anna cleared it with her mom. Friday night would work great. Now she just had to call Kari. As she reached for the phone, it rang.

"Hey, Anna." It was Sheryl. "You won't guess. Mike is having a bonfire in the field behind his house Friday night after the football game. Best part—we're invited."

Uh oh. Anna was silent. Nothing would be sweeter than a bonfire at Mike's, especially if the whole defensive line showed. Anna was so tempted.

There will always be temptations trying to pull us off heaven's highway. If we follow those side roads, however, we'll miss part of God's plan. Anna knew the Lord wanted her to be with Kari. He wanted to use her to reach out and comfort Kari, to cheer her up during this crummy time. Anna was going to have to choose: the bonfire or the Lord.

Temptations are always things that will draw us away from God's plan. When I was twenty-two, I interviewed to be a counselor of a Christian camp. While I was waiting to hear if I got the job, I met this guy. Nice guy. Cute guy. We had a lot in common and a lot of fun the two weeks we dated.

Then I heard from the Christian camp. I was hired! They wanted me there in a week—for the whole summer!

I had prayed I'd get the job. I already felt the Lord was leading me into youth ministry. Here was a chance to spend nine weeks with teens at a really cool camp. Horseback riding, swimming, campfires, Bible study, chapel. I knew it was God's plan.

Yet I wavered. I had just fallen into the arms of Mr. Romance. What if he was Mr. Right? What if this was my knight in shining armor, my future hubby? I could always be a camp counselor *next* summer.

I was trying to rationalize away the fact that I was being tempted. All the figuring and reasoning in the world wouldn't solve this. First of all, my infatuated heart was beating so loudly I could barely hear the Holy Spirit! Second, God *never* leads in two different directions at the same time! He wouldn't answer my prayer by opening the door at the camp AND introducing me to my future husband at the same time!

I'm afraid the guy was a side road temptation to pull me off of God's pathway, away from his plan. What did I do? I bit the bait. I veered off the road.

A few weeks later I was kicking myself! The guy dumped me. The camp had replaced me. I had the most miserable summer of my life. I had missed God's plan (boy, I'm glad he forgives us when we blow it!).

Temptations will always look good. Yet deep down inside, we usually know the right road to follow. God's road!

1. Jesus gives a hint for overcoming temptation. Read Luke 22:40–46. Prayer keeps us close to God so we can hear his voice. Pray for the wisdom and strength to make the right choice!

2. Where do temptations come from? They're not from God! Read James 1:13 and Matthew 4:1. When you feel tempted, recognize who the tempter is! Then what? Follow the advice in James 4:7.

3. What kind of temptation do you currently face? What do you think God wants you to do?

_____

_____

_____

_____

_____

_____

_____

If You Don't

STAND

for Something

You'll

FALL

for Anything.

STAND UP
FOR CHRIST!

DAY FOUR
Highway Patrol! Gotcha!

Derek slowly slipped in through the well-oiled door to the kitchen. He hoped to be as invisible as a vapor. He didn't want to run into his mom; she could always detect the mood on his face. She always read his body language as if it were painted in ten-foot-high letters!

But this time he'd fool her. As his mom entered the kitchen, her greeting startled Derek. He jerked up straight. The paper fell out of his pocket.

His face absolutely gave him away! His mom grabbed the paper. She knew something was up and she was right. A speeding ticket.

What rotten luck, Derek thought. *Nailed by the highway patrol and Mom on the same day.* Now he was really going to get it!

Discipline. It's a part of traveling through life that we may not enjoy, but we are wise to accept it! If we see discipline as punishment, we'll react negatively. True discipline is not punishment; it is training that corrects us, molds us, and perfects us.

God assigns parents the job of discipline. He assigns lawmakers the job of discipline. Teachers, coaches, cops—they all aim to discipline for the purpose of training us!

God disciplines us, too. He provides spiritual training that will keep us on the right road. Receiving discipline from the Lord with a humble and teachable attitude is very important. The Bible says it is a fool who resists correction, but that a wise man receives discipline. He more than receives it; he grows from it and is thankful for it!

When God trains us spiritually, it is proof of his love for us. God does not sit on his throne cracking a whip and laughing with delight. Instead, he sees we are about to head off in the wrong direction and steps in because he loves us.

Just so you know we're not making this up, let's go to the book of Hebrews and see what God's Word says.

Don't be discouraged when he has to show you where you are wrong. For when he punishes you, it proves that he loves you. . . . Let God train you. . . . should we not all the more cheerfully submit to God's training so that we can begin to really live? . . . God's correction is always right and for our best good. . . . Being punished isn't enjoyable while it is happening—it hurts! But afterwards we can see the result, a quiet growth in grace and character.

Hebrews 12:5–11

God's spiritual training proves his love. It also produces growth and character in us.

Now don't be thinking God is going to strike you with cancer if you lie to your teacher! He doesn't work like that. God's spiritual training means allowing you to suffer the consequences of your sins and rotten choices. Yes, he forgives you, but you still have to pay the price. Or he may use trials in your life to teach a spiritual lesson. He loves you enough to train you so you can grow spiritually. Receiving that training will help establish the curbs in life that keep you on the right road.

1. A good athlete knows that training for his sport will help him to be successful. God's spiritual training brings love, wisdom, security, and joy. Scope out these Scriptures: Revelation 3:19; Proverbs 3:11–12; Job 5:17. Are you mature and ready to accept the fact that spiritual discipline means God loves you?

   _____

   _____

   _____

2. God also gives parents the authority to discipline and train their children. Read Ephesians 6:1–4. Describe the parents' role. Define your role. How do you think God wants you to respond to your folks' discipline? Do you think obedience to parents is part of God's plan?

DAY FIVE
Watch for Oncoming Traffic!

There's a maniac loose on the road. Rumor has it he's headed your way. He's cruisin' toward you in the oncoming lane of traffic! His headlights will try to blind you. His swerving vehicle will attempt to run you off the road, straight into the ditch!

You need to be prepared. Keep your eyes straight ahead. Hold the wheel steady. Don't be edged off the road by his crafty schemes.

Sound familiar? Have you guessed who the dangerous driver is?

Satan, the one who rejected God's will during his days in heaven and was kicked down to earth. To this day, he still tries to lure others away from God.

He started with Adam and Eve, challenging God's command to not eat from the tree in the middle of the garden. Satan convinced Eve they would not die if they disobeyed (Genesis 3). Years later he turned to Jesus. He tried to twist the truth of God's Word (Luke 4:1–13).

If he lied to Adam and Eve, and took a swing at Jesus, surely he will attempt to trip you up as well.

Satan will try to confuse you. He will attempt to induce you to swerve off God's road by twisting Scripture, dangling temptations in front of you, and whispering his lies.

In order to be aware of the crafty schemes of Satan, you need to first know what his goals are and how he operates.

Satan has three main goals and they are all rotten!

Goal One: To lie and distort the truth.
John 8:44 calls Satan the father of lies. All he can do is lie. There is no truth in him.

Goal Two: To devour and discourage believers.
1 Peter 5:8 says Satan prowls around as a roaring lion looking for someone to pounce on, to tear apart!

Goal Three: To steal, kill, and destroy.
John 10:10 says it best: Satan wants to steal our joy, kill our trust, and destroy our relationship with Jesus. He may want to end our very lives, but Jesus said no one can snatch us out of God's hand (John 10:29).

Now you know Satan's goals. How does he try to achieve them? By disguising himself as a good guy with a sincere heart. The Bible says he comes as an angel of light. His schemes, lies, and temptations might look good at first glance, but they are a trap.

You can be wise to Satan's schemes by continually reading the truth in God's Word. When you know what is true, you'll be able to recognize what is false!

For example, when he whispers in your ear, "Go ahead, cuss that guy out for cutting in front of you," you'll know God's Word says, "let no unwholesome word proceed from your mouth" (Ephesians 4:29 NASB).

No matter how hard Satan tries to run you off the road, remember two things. First, Jesus, who is living in you, is greater and more powerful than Satan (1 John 4:4). Second, Jesus himself has prayed for your protection from "the evil one" (John 17:15). You would be wise to do the same! Then hold steady to the wheel, focusing your eyes on Jesus.

1. Paul, the apostle, wanted to journey to Thessalonica to preach to the growing church located there. But someone stopped him and his companions. Read 1 Thessalonians 2:18 to find out who. Satan cannot permanently block God's plans, yet can you recall a time he seemed to block them in your life?

   _____

   _____

2. Satan is always opposed to God's will. In fact, he has a will of his own. Read Isaiah 14:12–15. List the five things Satan says that he wanted to do.

   _____

   _____

   _____

   _____

   _____

3. Paul says in 2 Corinthians 2:11 we are not to be ignorant of Satan's schemes. Read the whole verse and find out why.

Instant Recall: *Knowing God's Word by Heart!*

1. To begin memorizing Scripture, select a verse that jumps out at you, one you *want* to remember, perhaps one that will help you in a current situation. These will be the easiest to memorize.

2. Know what the verse means by reading the verses around it (the context). See what a commentary has to say about it. Check the footnotes of your study Bible. Ask your pastor or youth leader.

3. Write the verse on a 3x5 card. First, write the reference (that's where it's located in the Bible), then the verse, then write the reference again. At the bottom write the topic of the verse. Your card should look like this:

---

1 John 4:7

Beloved, let us love one another, for love is from God; and every one who loves is born of God and knows God.

1 John 4:7

LOVE

Keep these cards together to create flash cards. You can also tape the one you're currently memorizing on your bathroom mirror or closet door.

4. Repeat the verse in your mind. Always say the reference, before and after the verse. It's great to hide the verse in your heart, but you also want to be able to find it in the Bible. Memorize the verse word for word.

5. Helpful hints: Write it, sing it, say it aloud, pray it, do it, visualize it on the page. Have a friend test you. Make it fun!

6. Review the verse over and over. This helps set it in your memory. Try selecting a special time for review, perhaps Sunday morning before church. Grab your flash cards, sit in a quiet place, and go for it! This also prepares your heart for church.

7. Set a goal. We suggest memorizing one verse a week—that's roughly four a month! Just think, by the end of the year, you can know fifty-two verses by heart!

WRONG WAY, DO NOT ENTER

Traveler's Advisory:
Roads to Avoid

DAY ONE
Danger Zones

The aquarium is one of our favorite places. The variety of sea life is incredible. You can even pet the baby sharks and stingrays.

Last time we visited, one particular fish captured our attention. Not only was it unique looking, it was doing strange things. The female was swimming near her babies. Whenever she sensed danger, she sucked the little ones into her mouth!

At first we thought she was eating them. But we continued to watch and saw that she released them when she felt it was safe. Her bizarre behavior was her way of protecting them!

God has his ways of protecting us, too. And though they may seem strange at first, they really do make sense! He wants to protect us because he loves us.

His Word warns us about specific roads to avoid, things not to get tangled up in. These are important things to pay attention to. Getting on the wrong road brings a ton of problems to life! When you're seeking God's direction in your life, you don't want to head in the wrong direction!

Knowing God's Word helps us to know good roads from bad roads. It provides clear instruction as to where to draw the line. The Word tells us not to be conformed to this world (Romans 12:1–2 NASB). James 4:4–5 alerts us to the fact that when we embrace the values of our culture we become a friend of the world and an enemy of God.

This happens so subtly. We start thinking things like, *One beer isn't bad, at least I'm not drunk.* Or, *Switching the price tag on these jeans is no big deal, this store makes lots of money.* How about, *Mom and Dad won't know I went to an R-rated flick; I'll tell them I saw that dumb PG movie.*

If we begin to accept the things our world says are okay, we'll compromise God's standards. We might decide God is just plain outdated. He's not up on all the stuff that's going on. He just wouldn't understand what it's like to be a teen today. WRONG!

He does know what it's like. That's why he gives us guidelines to follow.

God tells us to stay *off* the rotten roads. He tells us quite clearly what those are; it's up to us to listen to him! If we choose to take the wrong road, we'll have no one to blame but ourselves. We're quick to blame God when life gets bad, yet not everything that happens to us is God's fault. We have a free will; we are able to choose. We can decide to get off the road even when God flashes a neon sign reading, "WRONG WAY, DO NOT ENTER" right in front of our faces.

Rest assured that the second your big toe touches the wrong road, God springs into action! He will work to get you back on the right road (he loves you that much). Yet you must be willing to repent, turn from your mistakes, and jump back on the highway of God's way.

There will be times when it feels like you're on a deserted road. You may be standing alone but on the right road. Don't make a U-turn! Remember, Jesus was willing to stand alone for you, even to his death. When you stand for him, others will eventually see your light shine and join you. Your courage to take a stand for God's way will give other kids the courage to join you.

REST STOP, EXIT HERE

1. Look up Matthew 7:13–14. What is the difference between the wide road and the narrow road? Which is the Lord's road? Why do you think more people are on the wider road?

_____

_____

_____

_____

_____

_____

2. There is great reward for being on the right road and standing up for Christ. Read Matthew 10:32–33. What are some ways you and your friends can stand up for Christ on your campus?

_____

_____

_____

_____

DAY TWO
Soft Shoulders

He was a highly recruited basketball star in high school who went on to play pro ball for the Los Angeles Lakers and later moved to the Phoenix Suns. He's a six-foot-nine, physically fit, good-looking kinda guy. He's a Christian. And he's a virgin.

A. C. Green openly talks about his choice to remain sexually pure. In a recent interview he said he knows it's what God wants him to do, therefore that's what *he* wants to do, because it will make God happy. Not to mention that he wants to save his body for the person he'll spend his life with.

A. C. Green feels so strongly about reserving sex for marriage that he founded a group called Athletes for Abstinence. He's also produced a video with rap group Idol King called, "It Ain't Worth It."

And it ain't! Sex outside of marriage can result in so much pain: pregnancy, sexually transmitted diseases, AIDS, emotional turmoil, heartache, and the loss of self-respect.

Thanks to the True Love Waits campaign, hundreds of thousands of teens are making a commitment to abstinence. In one summer alone, more than five hundred thousand "purity pledges"—a covenant made between a teen, God, and a future spouse—were pounded into the ground on the mall in Washington, D.C. Such a pledge is a way of saying to a future husband or wife, "Hey, I was faithful to you even before I met you."

Fornication, sexual immorality, and adultery are all summed up as sexual relations outside of marriage. This is a road God's Word warns us over and over to avoid.

God's will is laid out plainly and simply in 1 Thessalonians 4:3: "For God wants you to be holy and pure, and to keep clear of all sexual sin so that each of you will marry in holiness and honor."

Very strong, direct words. Actually it sounds like he wants us to do more than just avoid it. It's more like—don't even think about it. No way. Not a chance. Nada! There is little to gain and much to lose. God desires to protect us from harm, keeping us walking with honor on his road.

So, are we saying don't even date? No. But date wisely. Be very picky about who you spend "alone" time with. Better yet, group date. It's more fun anyway. Plan active dates like tennis, bowling, or hiking. Talk a lot! Concentrate on getting to know that other person rather than getting into any touchy feely stuff.

Developing emotional intimacy is far better than the physical stuff. It makes you feel connected. Share your feelings, dreams, fears, hurts, and hopes with that special someone. It is a healthier, safer, and more godly way to give yourself to someone you care for.

Check into
True Love Waits
for yourself!
Call 1-800-LUV-WAIT

REST STOP, EXIT HERE

1. Check out these verses: 1 Corinthians 6:9, 13, 18, and 1 Thessalonians 4:1–8. In your own words, define God's will for your life concerning immorality.

_____

_____

_____

_____

_____

_____

2. There is strength in numbers! Call the True Love Waits headquarters. See how you can start a campaign at your church or school. Pray for God to give you courage, wisdom, and faith as you step out to represent him.

3. Brainstorm on some creative great date ideas. Record your ideas so you don't forget them. Then check out the book, *258 Great Dates While You Wait* by Susie Shellenberger and Greg Johnson.

DAY THREE
D.W.I.

The Monday morning buzz.

"Oh, my gosh, I had the biggest hangover this weekend—you would not believe!"

"You won't guess what happened to Mandy. She was so wasted she ended up with this guy in the back of somebody's car. She didn't even know who he was."

"Did you hear that Kevin downed a fifth and smoked pot Friday night? The guys left him at the park and someone saw him and called 911. The hospital called his parents. He's in so much trouble."

Beer, wine, mixed drinks, wine coolers, hard liquor, pot, cocaine, heroin. Every teen alive, including you, will be faced with alcohol and drugs at some point: junior high, high school, college. It's illegal. It's dangerous. It's not part of God's best for us. It never, ever leads to anything good. Listen to some wise words from Proverbs:

> Whose heart is filled with anguish and sorrow? Who is always fighting and quarreling? Who is the man with bloodshot eyes and many wounds? It is the one who spends long hours in the taverns, trying out new mixtures. Don't let the sparkle and the smooth taste of strong wine deceive you. For in the end it bites like a poisonous serpent; it stings like an adder. You will see hallucinations and have delirium tremens, and you will say foolish, silly things that would embarrass you no end when sober.
>
> Proverbs 23:29–33

Wine gives false courage; hard liquor leads to brawls;
what fools men are to let it master them, making them
reel drunkenly down the street!

Proverbs 20:1

Drugs and alcohol are a road for losers. Yet teens still
drink. Why? For lots of different reasons. Maybe they want
to numb out, escape, or lessen the pain. For some it's
intended to help them lighten up or party hearty, thinking
it's a blast. Others want to fit in, be part of the group. Then
there are those who are angry inside and use it to blow off
steam. Yet alcohol and drugs don't solve a person's problems. They usually make them worse.

But what about Christian teens? Research shows that
kids in the kingdom are gulping down the "brewskis," too.
Bill and I have seen lots of youth group kids fall into the
drinking trap. Why?

We believe it's because they are forgetting who they are.
They are children of God himself, transferred out of Satan's
kingdom into God's! They are seated in heavenly places
with Christ, able to come into God's presence with confidence. They are greatly loved by a heavenly Father willing
to give his only Son's life to buy them back and provide forgiveness for their sin, a Father who will help them through
every tough time. They are chosen, holy, set apart for God's
purposes. They are royalty, made to be kings and priests
before the Lord (Revelation 1:6 KJV).

Proverbs 31:4 (NASB) states that it is not for kings to drink
wine or for rulers to desire strong drink. Romans 13:13–14
instructs, "Don't spend your time in wild parties and getting drunk. . . . But ask the Lord Jesus Christ to help you
live as you should, and don't make plans to enjoy evil."

When that beer or joint is passed your way, will you forget who you are in Christ or remember that you are a child
of an awesome God?

REST STOP, EXIT HERE

1. God wants us to avoid the road of alcohol. Christians are not to be loaded and wasted with liquor or drugs; we are to be filled with something more wonderful. Read Ephesians 5:18. Describe the difference between joy from the Holy Spirit and the buzz provided by alcohol.

_____

_____

_____

_____

2. Many Scriptures talk about being sober. Check out these verses: 1 Thessalonians 5:4–8; 2 Timothy 4:5; 1 Peter 4:7; 5:8. List the different reasons we are to be sober.

_____

_____

_____

_____

_____

_____

DAY FOUR
Tow Away Zone

Lauren could hardly wait for the end of each month. She searched the mailbox with excitement. At last! Her teen magazine had arrived. She instantly opened to the back to discover her fate in the horoscope column. Her finger quickly slid down the page to Aries, to read of her destiny. Can the stars truly predict what will happen in Lauren's life?

Matt was spending the night at Sean's house. As they flipped through the channels, there it was. Incredible. The lady on the stage was calling people out of the audience and telling them true things about themselves! Then she was forecasting their future. Awesome. Was it real? Could so-called psychics really know stuff about people? Was it God's power or Satan's?

Sarah took her normal seat in biology class unaware of what the day's lesson would be. The teacher instructed the students to put their heads down, close their eyes, and begin to breath deeply.

Soon they were to picture themselves on the beach, then floating like a cloud over the vast ocean. They were instructed to leave their bodies and go deep into the ocean to find the great dolphin. There they could ask this wise dolphin any question and it would tell them what to do. They were told they could rely on him alone. They didn't need their parents (and certainly not God). Who was this dolphin's voice that spoke?

Luke left the store wearing his newly purchased six-sided crystal. He had heard that it had incredible healing and energizing powers. He was anxious to see if it were true. Did that piece of quartz really possess powers?

Is there more to these examples than what meets the eye? You better believe there is!

These are examples of New Age practices that lead people away from Christianity and the one true God.

The New Age Movement is a popular and powerful influence today. It is a vague combination of occultic (Satanic) and Eastern religious beliefs (Hindu). New Age practices, terms, and beliefs have crept into everything from movies to music (the dreamy sounding instrumentals used for mind trips, meditation, and self-hypnosis) to jewelry (six-sided crystals, zodiac and yin-yang symbols, mood rings, eyeballs) to exercise (yoga). People dabble with some of these seemingly harmless practices and before they know it, they've been taken in and towed away!

God makes his point clear when he says, "You shall worship the Lord your God and serve Him only" (Luke 4:8 NASB). He also declares, "For I am God, and there is no other; I am God, and there is no one like Me" (Isaiah 46:9 NASB). There is only *one* true God!

As Christians looking for direction in life, we can go to a real God, who is all-knowing and all-powerful. We are *not* to consult psychics, horoscopes, tarot cards, deceased spirits, Ouija boards, or palm readers (Leviticus 19:31). Our faith and trust are to be in Jesus.

Jesus assures us when he says, "I am the way, and the truth, and the life" (John 14:6 NASB). In Christ we find direction, truth, hope, healing, and abundant life.

As Christians, we are to run from any roads that get us headed in any direction other than God's! We are to keep our eyes and hearts set on Jesus! Stay close to him and you won't be led astray.

REST STOP, EXIT HERE

1. One of the central New Age teachings is called moral relativism. This means there is no right or wrong, no sin, no good or bad, but whatever you want to do and believe is okay for you. This is a lie. Why do you think Satan wants people to believe this? If there is no sin, do people need Jesus?

_____

_____

_____

_____

2. Reincarnation is the New Age belief that people have many lives. It teaches that at death the spirit reenters a new body or an animal and continues to live. Read Hebrews 9:27 and Ecclesiastes 3:1–2 to find out the truth. How many times are we born? How many times do we die? (Remember, the Christian's spirit goes to heaven, the non-Christian's to hell.) Don't be fooled. Read up on the New Age Movement in _From Nirvana to the New Age_ by Mary Ann Lind, published by Revell.

DAY FIVE
House of . . . Grunge?

Andrea

A-a-a-chew! Dust. Dust on the TV. Dust on the picture frames. Dust on the dogs. Dust on the bubble gum machine on the corner of my desk. I hate dust. And I hate to clean house. But if I don't try to keep up, we'll be hauling Bill's leaf blower in here just to blast a trail through this place.

Fact is, houses get dirty. All houses. Even you. Huh? That's right. The Bible says your body is the temple (or house) of the Holy Spirit. Every time you open the door to things that are offtrack and unclean, a little more dirt blows in.

Consider the TV. It brings all kinds of dust in. The sex scenes on lusty shows like *Melrose Place* or soap operas. The violence on *Top Cops* or *NYPD Blue*. These are like the mildew that lurks in the corners of damp places; the more you watch, the more it grows.

How about music? Raunchy song lyrics and music videos are like spider webs hanging in every corner. Then there are steamy romance novels and magazine articles and pornography creating a layer of dust that dulls the appearance of a once shiny, clean house.

Little by little, the house of the Holy Spirit becomes the house of grunge!

Is your house in need of a cleanup? The Bible tells us to watch over our hearts with diligence. That means to be very picky about what you allow to get inside of you. Be aware of what you choose to expose yourself to.

Listen up. You can't get toothpaste back in the tube. Similarly you can't undo things you've seen, heard, or read. Of course, you can ask for forgiveness, but play offense—plan ahead!

The dust we allow to blow into our houses creates problems. Seductive and romantic scenes can produce impure thoughts and desires. Horror, mystery, or violent stuff can cause us to feel fearful, worried, or revengeful. None of these are God's best for us.

Bad thoughts can lead to bad actions. Bottom line: All this trash ends up stealing our peace and joy. Why risk it?

God wants us to run from lust. He wants us to be free from worry and fear by trusting him. He wants us to be forgiving toward others, not plotting revenge or evil. He wants us to have peace and joy.

Since your body is Christ's home, you need to be on the lookout. Lots of opportunities to expose yourself to filth will come knocking at your door. Do yourself a favor. Check the peephole before you turn that knob.

Listen Up! Here are a bunch of other roads screaming, **Wrong Way, Do Not Enter!**

- Hot-headed anger (Proverbs 15:1–2)
- Revenge (Romans 12:17–21)
- Hanging with the wrong friends (1 Corinthians 15:33)
- Blowin' off the law (1 Peter 2:13–14)
- Abortion (Exodus 20:13; Proverbs 31:8–9)
- Being a lazy couch potato (Proverbs 20:13; 15:19)
- Gossiping (Proverbs 11:13; 16:28)
- Selfishness (Philippians 2:3–5; Ephesians 2:10)
- Homosexuality (1 Corinthians 6:9–10)
- Disobeying your parents (Ephesians 6:1–3)
- Telling white lies (Proverbs 6:16–17; Colossians 3:9)
- Astrology (Isaiah 47:13–14)
- Witchcraft, magic (Deuteronomy 18:9–14)
- Swearing (Ephesians 4:29; Proverbs 4:24)
- Being prideful (James 4:6; 1 Peter 5:6)
- Doing what everyone else does (Romans 12:1–2)

Ten Teachings from God

Check Out These Roads to AVOID!

1. **You shall have no other gods before me.**
   Worship him only!

2. **You shall not have any idols.**
   Make God #1 in your life.

3. **You shall not take the name of the Lord your God in vain.**
   Use his name carefully.

4. **You shall remember the Sabbath day and keep it holy.**
   Rest and go to worship on God's day.

5. **You shall honor your father and mother.**
   They are special folks; respect them.

6. **You shall not murder.**
   Respect the lives of other people.

7. **You shall not commit adultery.**
   Keep your marriage pure.

8. **You shall not steal.**
   Take only what belongs to you.

9. **You shall not lie.**
   Tell the truth.

10. **You shall not covet your neighbor's house, etc.**
    Be happy with what you have.

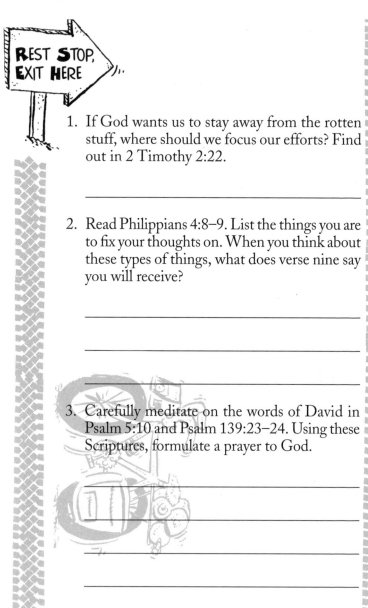

REST STOP, EXIT HERE

1. If God wants us to stay away from the rotten stuff, where should we focus our efforts? Find out in 2 Timothy 2:22.

   _____

2. Read Philippians 4:8–9. List the things you are to fix your thoughts on. When you think about these types of things, what does verse nine say you will receive?

   _____

   _____

   _____

3. Carefully meditate on the words of David in Psalm 5:10 and Psalm 139:23–24. Using these Scriptures, formulate a prayer to God.

   _____

   _____

   _____

   _____

FALLING ROCK

When Bad Stuff Topples on God's Guys!

DAY ONE
Bumpy Ride!

Bill

Twenty-three teens tightened their helmets, checked their chains, and secured their waterbottles as we began day three of a two-hundred-mile bike trip down Highway 1 on the scenic California coastline. With perfectly pressured tires, we were totally ready for the terrain. That day's route would be taking us through traffic lights and city streets.

The group tried to stay evenly spaced, but a traffic jam on the bike path forced my bike out onto a busy street. Caught between the cars and the curb, I couldn't swerve to avoid the drainage grate that was suddenly in front of me. The bars of the grate were just wide enough for my one-inch racing tires to drop down, sending me over the top of the handlebars. A badly bent wheel and a battered and bruised shoulder sent me hunting for the nearest repair shop and first aid kit.

Tough break. There was no way I could have prevented or prepared for the wreck. Often as we travel the road of life, rotten things happen: falling rocks—just as we pass by.

Divorce, death of a loved one, earthquakes, misunder-
standings, illness, shattered dreams, layoffs, bad report cards.
Some things seem like plain ol' bad breaks. Others are due
to bad people. And many of the rocks that fall on us do so
because we pried them loose ourselves with bad choices.

Let's admit it. Stuff happens. Bad stuff.

The bad thing about bad things is that they don't care
who they land on! It doesn't hinge on whether you are a
good person or a crummy person. It's not based on whether
you deserve it or not. And bad stuff happening to you does
not mean you are out of God's plan!

Take Job, for instance. The Bible says he was blameless.
He was a fair man. An upstanding citizen. He honored God
with his life. Still, he got dumped on—lost his home, his
animals, his children, his health. Did he deserve it? NO. Was
he out of God's will? NO (see the Book of Job).

Matthew 5:45 tells us it rains on the just and the unjust,
the good and the bad, the righteous and the unrighteous,
Christians and non-Christians. Life isn't fair. That's a fact.
Some people seem to experience more rain than others.
Some get showers while others get thunderstorms!

Too bad it doesn't work like the meal tickets at school.
We could each get a card with ten "rotten break" circles.
With each negative occurrence we get a circle punched.
When our card is full, it's over. No more bad things, only
good. We'd be waving those cards in the air, high as we
could, saying, "Look God, my card is full. I'm all punched
out. You can make it stop now."

But even Jesus tells us to expect trials and troubles in this
life (read it for yourself in John 16:33). Why? We live in a
fallen world full of imperfect people and broken dreams.
Earth is Satan's domain, full of evil things. Only heaven
promises no pain, no tears, no evil.

Being a Christian doesn't guarantee easy sailing on the
sea of life. The apostle Paul suffered imprisonment, beat-

ings, shipwreck, rejection, and hunger. Stephen was stoned. John the Baptist was beheaded. Moses was separated from his family. Ruth lost her husband. Mary had to watch her son die. Jonah was in the belly of the whale (okay, that was his own fault). All of those people were God's children, and they still had tough times.

When I was in college, my father died suddenly from a heart attack. That was very hard for me. Another hard thing has been that Andrea and I are unable to have children.

We know that Christians are not exempt from rocks falling on them! We will not be shielded from bad things. God doesn't give us umbrellas to keep the rain from pouring down on our heads; he more often gives us towels to dry each other off after the storms. To help us carry each other's loads. To be encouragers. Part of our calling as Christians is to "bear one another's burdens."

The Bible doesn't guarantee a fairy-tale life, but it does guarantee that the Lord himself will give us the strength, comfort, and perseverance we'll need to continue the race. Whether our trial is a hundred-yard dash or an eight-hundred-meter race, he will enable us to endure when we turn to him alone.

Prayer Power

When calamity comes, carve out some specific time to spend alone with God. Prayer puts you in the position to hear from God. Tune in to what the Holy Spirit is saying to you. Allow him to soften your heart and be accepting of the trials you face. Ask him to show you his plan. Ask him to give you wisdom. He promises to give wisdom to his kids in James 1:5. Prayer fills you with his power!

1. Does God know when you're troubled? Does he care? Read Psalm 34:18 to find out.

2. Romans 8:28 in *The Living Bible* says "that all that happens to us is working for our good if we love God and are fitting into his plans." What are the two conditions for it all working out for our good? What if we turn our back on God and purposely choose to get off his path for us? Do you think God is obligated to work things together for our good?

_____

_____

_____

3. Read Matthew 7:24–27. When the storms of life thunder down on you, which foundation will sustain you? Who does the "rock" represent and what difference does it make in your life?

_____

_____

DAY TWO
Your Traveling Companion

Sean sprinted to Algebra class from his girlfriend's home-room, where he had delivered the notebook she'd left in his car. Mr. Owens, the Mathematical Monarch, refused to dismiss Sean's three minutes of tardiness. He pronounced his sentence: detention. Sean wanted to land a left hook on Owens's jaw. It was Sean's third detention that semester, meaning he'd be suspended from the basketball team. "God, I thought you were on my side," he said accusingly.

Kylee finally found the perfect dress for the dance. Soft pink, with lots of lace. As she took it from the bag and pre-pared to model it for her mom, she found the security tag still attached. When she returned to the store, the tag set off the security alarms. She had no receipt. No proof. She was booked on a shoplifting charge. "God, this can't be hap-pening. I thought you loved me."

Ben was devastated. He knew his brother, Gary, was going through hard times, but he never suspected that he had sunk so low. The empty bottle of pills lay on the floor; Gary had overdosed. He was gone. A senseless tragedy. Ben screamed into his tear-soaked pillow, "Where were you, God?"

Have you ever experienced a situation that left you shak-ing your fist at God? Ever wonder the purpose behind God's seeming silence? Maybe you've felt God stopped loving you, like Sean and Kylee did. Or you may have felt abandoned, like Ben. It's okay to rattle the gates of heaven, wondering where God is. He feels your frustration and your need to understand. But it's *only* okay as long as you stop to realize that he does love you and is still at your side. Even when things look disastrous, *God is still with you.* He's the perfect traveling companion.

Need some proof?

Peer into Daniel's life for a second. He was thrown into a den of lions for refusing to worship the king. But God sent an angel to shut the lions' mouths (Daniel 6). His buddies Shadrach, Meshack, and Abednego were sent into a fiery furnace, yet the Lord kept the fire from consuming them (Daniel 3).

Can it get much worse than facing death in a den of lions or risk being turned to ashes in a blazing inferno? The point is not that they faced tough stuff, but that *God was with them.* He never abandoned them, nor will he abandon us. He never cuts off his flow of love.

When the hurricanes of life hit, you may not feel the Lord *at your side* because you are *in his arms!* It's true! There will be times when he will carry you through the tough stuff. He will *never* abandon you.

If you let this truth breeze over your head and insist that God has left you and doesn't love you anymore, then you can't help but be angry and blame him every time life goes wacky and throws you a curve ball. BEWARE! Anger is a relationship shredder!

Anger creates a wall between you and God. When you're angry at God you can't fully love him or let him love you. Blaming him makes it impossible to praise him. When you put the brakes on praise and thanksgiving, you lose your joy. Then you lose your strength to keep going. The joy of the Lord is your strength. Anger and blame blow out your flame of joy.

So, what are you to do when you are seething inside? The healthiest way to get rid of anger is to be mad at the situation—blame the circumstances instead of targeting yourself, your friends, or your God.

Jesus assured his disciples, before he left for heaven, that he would never leave them or forsake them. The same promise holds true for you and me!

Silent Partner

Don't mistake God's silence! Whether we like it or not, God answers prayer according to *his* timetable.

He may delay answering because there are circumstances he is changing. He may wait to answer because he is trying to prepare *us* for his answer! If God has not answered, it is because he is not done working!

If he doesn't answer the way you expected, wake up! Pay attention! He's trying to show you his plan!

It's important not to lose your faith while you're waiting for God to make his move. Kicking and screaming, sobbing and swearing won't speed God along. Such behavior only shows your faith is floundering and your patience is wearing thin.

Strengthen your faith while the clock ticks away according to God's timing. Keep reading the Word. Keep asking, seeking, and knocking. Rest in the fact that God loves you and he's promised never to leave you high and dry.

Trust him. His answers on *his* timetable will be perfect. You will see his glory, if you believe.

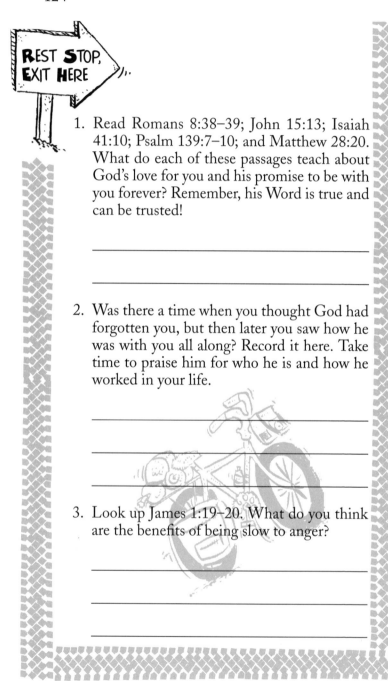

REST STOP, EXIT HERE

1. Read Romans 8:38–39; John 15:13; Isaiah 41:10; Psalm 139:7–10; and Matthew 28:20. What do each of these passages teach about God's love for you and his promise to be with you forever? Remember, his Word is true and can be trusted!

   _____

   _____

2. Was there a time when you thought God had forgotten you, but then later you saw how he was with you all along? Record it here. Take time to praise him for who he is and how he worked in your life.

   _____

   _____

   _____

3. Look up James 1:19–20. What do you think are the benefits of being slow to anger?

   _____

   _____

   _____

DAY THREE
Explain Yourself, God!

Andrea

I stood outside the intensive care unit of Hillcrest Hospital, numb with grief. My family was gathered, crying, some doubled over in agony. My thirty-five-year-old sister Allison, who had suffered from a sudden and severe infection, had just been pronounced dead. She was the one I shared a room with growing up, the one I was with in the choir and school plays. We whispered our secrets deep into the night while we were in college; we even had a crush on the same guy. We prayed together and passed praise tapes back and forth. Now she was gone.

My numbness turned to simmering disbelief. "Lord, how could you let this happen? She was so young. She had little Katie Marie and her husband," I reminded God. "Some things I can let go," I snapped, "but this one, Lord, you *have* to explain to me."

But heaven was silent. Days later, I heard someone say that God does not owe us explanations for what he allows to happen in our lives. At first that ticked me off. But as I chewed on it, I knew they were right.

I thought of Isaiah 55:8–9 (NASB), where the Lord says:

"For My thoughts are not your thoughts,
Neither are your ways My ways," declares the LORD.
"For as the heavens are higher than the earth,
So are My ways higher than your ways,
And My thoughts than your thoughts."

And then Proverbs 25:2 (NASB) states that "it is the glory of God to conceal a matter."

The truth that God knows better than me and he has a right to keep his purposes and ways to himself began to sink in.

After all, he is God.

And as his children, we need to trust him. Proverbs 3:5–6 tells us to trust the Lord with our whole hearts and not to depend on our ability to understand the situation. Don't expect to have all the answers. Don't expect everything to make sense!

Picture Joseph sitting in a prison cell, falsely accused of trying to rape Potiphar's wife (Genesis 39). The Bible doesn't say that God sent Joseph an angel to explain the plan to him. Yet God *did* have a plan and he was busy making it all work—even when it certainly didn't look like it to Joseph.

God always has a plan. God always makes sense! It's just that we may not understand it all until we get to heaven, until we get to sit down face-to-face with Jesus!

In one of his letters to the Corinthians, Paul stated:

> In the same way, we can see and understand only a little about God now, as if we were peering at his reflection in a poor mirror; but someday we are going to see him in his completeness, face to face. Now all that I know is hazy and blurred, but then I will see everything clearly, just as clearly as God sees into my heart right now.
>
> 1 Corinthians 13:12

Without knowing the whole story, Paul continued to love God. So did Joseph. So do I. What about you?

We only see a piece of life at a time; God sees the whole picture. We see a section of the movie; God sees it from the opening scene clear through to the closing credits! Often with time, we begin to understand. Many times, we don't. The reasons you didn't make cheerleader, your grandpa died, your brother is ill, your dog got hit—these may never be clear. The crucial question is, are you willing to trust God 100 percent even without an explanation from the throne room?

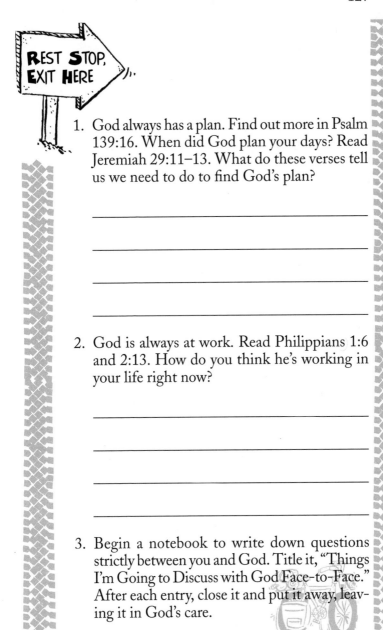

1. God always has a plan. Find out more in Psalm 139:16. When did God plan your days? Read Jeremiah 29:11–13. What do these verses tell us we need to do to find God's plan?

_____

_____

_____

_____

2. God is always at work. Read Philippians 1:6 and 2:13. How do you think he's working in your life right now?

_____

_____

_____

_____

3. Begin a notebook to write down questions strictly between you and God. Title it, "Things I'm Going to Discuss with God Face-to-Face." After each entry, close it and put it away, leaving it in God's care.

DAY FOUR
Hang On to Heaven!

Andrea

Paul knelt on the dusty ground as the sun dipped below the horizon, spraying colors of pink, orange, purple, and blue across the sky. Exhausted and confused, he was asking the Lord for the third time to remove from him what he called his "thorn in the flesh."

After all, Paul was a faithful servant of Jesus Christ. He preached day in and day out. He prayed for others and they were healed. He endured trials every moment of his life. But this thorn persisted.

God's response was not what Paul would have chosen. "My grace is sufficient for you, for my power is made perfect in weakness" (2 Corinthians 12:9 NIV). Instead of releasing Paul from his pain, God granted him grace. God shows his power through our weaknesses. When we are weak, *he* can make us stronger. Grace is God's unearned favor and kindness that helps us get through our trial. It's strength, courage, and patience. I personally define grace as God's incredible superglue sent down from the throne room to hold us together in situations where normally we would not be able to bear one more ounce of hurt. It is a supernatural sustaining substance!

Yet grace is only supplied if we hang on to heaven, if we stay plugged in to God!

My grandmother Elizabeth has a sign on the back of her front door that says:

> There is nothing that will happen today, that God and I can't handle together!

Every time she prepares to leave her home, those words hang as a reminder that when you put your hand in the Lord's, one way or another, you're going to make it!

You've heard the phrase "abide in the vine." Have you discovered what that truly means? Let's define it in reverse. What happens when a branch is cut off from the main vine? It shrivels up and dies. Is it being fed and nourished by the vine? NO. Can that branch produce fruit? NO. Can that branch be controlled by the vine? NO. Can the branch depend on the vine? NO, NO, and NO again!

There is a flow of life from the vine that surges through the branches. God is the vine; we are the branches and we are interconnected with God; we are one with him!

It is an intimate bond. Personal. Real. Alive.

Having this lifeline to God gives us what we need to keep going. It gives us the grace to look to the future with hope and joy.

Paul states in Philippians 3:13 that one thing he has learned to do is forget the past and look forward to what lies ahead. You can't change the fact that something has happened; not even God will rewrite the past. But you can cast your cares on the Lord and keep moving forward!

Hebrews 12:1–2 encourages us to run with patience the particular race that God has set before us, keeping our eyes on Jesus. He is our leader and our instructor.

When life has hardships, focus on Jesus! You can choose how you'll respond to crisis and disappointments in your life.

We urge you: No matter the type of rock or the weight of the boulder that so rudely interrupts your life, above all else, DON'T LET GO OF GOD!

130

REST STOP, EXIT HERE

1. Abide in the vine! What example for staying in touch with God did Jesus give us in Luke 6:12? Select a "mountain" you can retreat to, a quiet, private place to be alone with your heavenly Father every day.

2. Read Psalm 121:1–8. List at least five things the Lord will do for those who trust in him. Which one is most valuable to you today?

_____

_____

_____

_____

_____

3. There are two lifesaving qualities the Lord promises to give his children that will help them in tough times. Find out what they are in Romans 15:5. In which situations that you face right now could you use a little of each quality?

_____

_____

DAY FIVE
Bad Stuff Gone Good

Mold. A fuzzy fungus growing proudly on rotting food or decaying matter. Could anything good come from such disgusting stuff?

Yeah, HEALING!

Huh?

Penicillin is an antibiotic that kills harmful microorganisms in our bodies that cause illness. Ready for this? Penicillin is produced by a GREEN MOLD! Yipes!

And to think, God planned it that way!

God is an expert at bringing good out of bad. Joseph told his evil and jealous brothers who sold him into slavery, "God turned into good what you meant for evil, for he brought me to this high position I have today so that I could save the lives of many people" (Genesis 50:20). Oh, yeah. He was the same guy who was in prison earlier. Boy, what a life!

Lee Ezell was eighteen when she was raped by a salesman with whom she worked. A short time later she discovered she was pregnant. Lee tried to explain the horrible truth to her mother, but her mother accused her of lying and kicked her out of the house.

God provided a loving couple for Lee to live with until the baby was born. She gave the child up for adoption, asking the Lord to place her in a Christian home. Lee felt a piece of her was missing, and thought often of her child.

Twenty-one years later Lee got an unexpected phone call. It was her daughter, Julie. She had been raised by a wonderful couple but wanted to find her birth mother. They now enjoy a close, loving relationship.

Pretty extreme, but it's true.

Romans 8:28 assures us "that all that happens to us is working together for our good if we love God and are fitting into his plans."

We may not understand why we suffer, and we will not be able to control every single thing that happens to us. Yet if we love the Lord and aim to do his will, he can turn pain and misfortune into opportunities for growth. What possible good can be born from bad?

Hang with us and we'll take a look.

Positive Products of Suffering

1. Suffering teaches us to be sensitive and compassionate, being able to comfort others who are going through hard times (read 2 Corinthians 1:3–5).

2. Problems and trials teach us to be patient, which leads to strong character (read Romans 5:3–4).

3. God can use negatives to create in us the positive qualities of Jesus (read Colossians 3:10; Romans 8:29; Galatians 5:22).

4. Crises can cause us to reevaluate our lives and recognize our need for God (read Job 2:7–10).

5. Tough stuff can test and develop our faith so we will be pleasing to God and able to withstand the storms of life (read James 1:2–4; Hebrews 11:6).

Convinced? Suffering really can become a meaningful, purposeful experience if we allow the Lord to weave it into something beautiful.

In the weaving of our lives, the Lord uses the dark threads of hard times to complement the colorful threads of good times. Together they create a brilliant design that otherwise would not be possible.

REST STOP, EXIT HERE

1. Look up each Scripture under "Positive Products of Suffering" on page 132. Identify tough times in your life that produced these results in you. Thank the Lord for each one.

   _____

   _____

2. In his closing remarks to the Ephesians, Paul asks them for prayer. Though he's sitting in prison, chained to a Roman guard, he doesn't want prayer for his release. Read Ephesians 6:19–20. What did Paul request? How do you think it witnesses to others when we are going through hard times, yet continue to speak out and love the Lord?

   _____

   _____

3. Hard times are part of the Christian life. Being a godly person will include suffering. Read 1 Peter 2:20–21. How does suffering for doing the right thing help to train you spiritually?

   _____

   _____

Do's and Don'ts of Helping a Friend through a Tough Time

- Do let him know you care! Tell him, hug him, be there! Send him a card with an encouraging Bible verse.
- Do spend time just listening to her talk out her feelings and hash out the situation. Hey, even you guys need to verbalize your inner wrestling matches.
- Do keep your advice to yourself (in most cases)!
- Do pray for him and with him. Ask him how you can best pray for him, what he feels he needs (such as strength, wisdom, peace). For some situations, the best way to pray is for God's will to be done since neither you nor your friend may know what is actually best.
- Do take him walking or go shoot some hoops. Physical exercise can lift a person's spirits and even help him think more clearly. It won't solve the problem or heal a deep hurt, but it does release energizers into the blood stream.
- Do alert a parent, pastor, teacher, or counselor if your friend talks of feeling hopeless, purposeless, and says that she has no reason to live. Your friend may be thinking of suicide. Watch for changes in her eating and sleeping pattern, a drop in grades, and a changed personal appearance.
- Don't tell him you know how he feels. Unless you've been through the same exact thing, you *can't* know how he feels. Besides, we all respond differently to situations. Say, "I don't understand exactly what you're going through, but I'm here for you."
- Don't share a similar problem with her or tell her a story about someone you know who had something

similar happen! "Man, you think you have it bad, when I was in the fifth grade . . ." This really won't comfort your friend. It only makes her feel like you don't think her situation is any big deal.

• Don't tell him it will get better! As much as you both may want it, you can't peer into the future and know what is around the corner. You can, however, remind your friend that God is faithful and trustworthy. Keep him looking to God.

DANGEROUS CURVES AHEAD

Trusting God in Unknown Territory

DAY ONE
Curvy Roads

Andrea

The San Marcos pass struck me as a trail of terror the first few times I drove it from the Santa Ynez valley over to beautiful Santa Barbara, California. Everyone told me the pass was a shortcut over the mountain. Well, technically, it may be fewer miles, but if you drive it the speed of a scared snail, believe me, it's no shortcut!

The twists and turns in the road were incredible. The curves around the side of the mountain. The cliffs that dropped straight down. The steep inclines and swift declines. It was roller-coaster terrain.

Life can drag us down some pretty tough terrain, too! There are ups and downs, valleys and mountain tops. With all the twists and turns, curves and cliffs, you can't always see what's up ahead. You don't know what to expect. You

136

don't know how to prepare. Is there any way to straighten the road?

Yes! Step by step. How? By trusting the Lord!

Listen up:

> Trust the Lord with all your heart,
> And do not lean on your own understanding.
> In all your ways acknowledge Him,
> And He will make your paths straight.
>
> Proverbs 3:5–6 NASB

There it is. The Lord will work in your life to straighten the path before you. But there are some definite prerequisites! You need to do your part, then God will do his! Here's your to-do list:

1. **Totally Trust God!**
   Trust is the key. It means to put your confidence in God, depending on him for whatever you need. Notice it says to trust with *all* of your heart. Not a quarter. Not half. Not seven-eighths. Your whole heart, 100 percent! No doubting allowed. No worrying allowed.

2. **Do Not Lean on Yourself!**
   That's right. Don't rely on yourself to understand everything that happens and what it means. Stop trying to figure it all out. Leave it in God's hands. He's got all the facts. He sees the big picture. You don't.

3. **Acknowledge Him in Everything!**
   This is a big one. Put God first in everything. First in every decision, every plan, every everything! Consult him. Do what he would want you to do.

Now, God's part: He will make your paths straight!

That means he will guide you, direct you, show you the way. It doesn't mean he will make the road smooth. It does

mean he will tell you how to travel the road so you get over the mountains and through the valleys.

You will still have curves ahead. That's life. But the spot where you are about to put your foot will be straight as you trust the Lord. He will guide you step by step when you trust him completely.

REST STOP, EXIT HERE

1. Sometimes trusting God completely sounds too scary. Write a prayer telling God your fears and concerns about trusting him wholeheartedly. Then ask him to release you from those doubts, filling you with trust.

_____

_____

2. Now that you have those fears out of the way, think about and list all the pluses to relying on God and not on yourself.

_____

_____

3. Think of one simple thing you could do to put God first and acknowledge him in these areas:

Home_____

School_____

Church_____

Work_____

Free Time_____

DAY TWO
Enjoy the Ride

Bill

Trusting the Lord is an adventure. Day by day, year by year, you watch to see what he's up to. Where will he take you next? Who will he bring into your life? What does he have planned for your vocation? When you truly rely on the Lord, you can relax, sit back, and enjoy the ride.

The best part of trusting God is that you can live without fear of the future. Sure, the future is unknown. Some people get whacked out, being afraid of what is up ahead. But with God in charge, we don't have to be worrywarts or fearful fellows. God always has it all worked out.

For four long, hot summers, I worked for the Department of Transportation in Iowa. The first few years, I was stationed out on country roads. My only responsibility was to count cars. It was great. As I sat there waiting for cars, I caught some rays, drank lots of Mountain Dew, and studied for a correspondence course I was taking. I even read the whole New Testament right there on the job.

When summer rolled around again, I applied for the job for the fifth time. I didn't get hired. I couldn't believe it! All those years of faithful service. I was always on time, always honest, always respectful. I never even took advantage of the expense account! A totally clean track record, and I was turned down for the job.

Anger surfaced. I was mad at God for days. How was I going to earn money for tuition? How was I going to be able to save up to support myself the next year in seminary? I reacted in anger and fear (I've learned a lot about trusting since then).

After a week of wondering what I was going to do, I got a call from an elderly man in a small farm town close to my home. He asked if I would pray about coming to be the student pastor at their church. They were a small congregation without a permanent pastor.

I immediately knew this was what God had planned. I said yes. It turned out to be a fabulous summer. I learned a lot about the ministry and made several special friendships. God even provided the money I needed for my first year of seminary.

I have learned since then that God always has a plan. I don't need to panic or worry or fear for the future. Neither do you! When we trust God, our lives will show it. We will be confident in him!

Trusting God takes guts. You can do it. He'll never let you down. He may make you wait or do things you didn't plan to do, but he is trustworthy. So sit back, relax, and enjoy the ride. God has your future all figured out.

All I Have Seen Teaches Me to Trust the Creator for All I Have Not Seen

Ralph Waldo Emerson

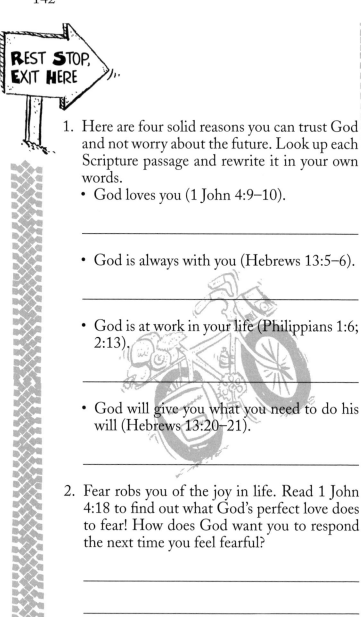

REST STOP, EXIT HERE

1. Here are four solid reasons you can trust God and not worry about the future. Look up each Scripture passage and rewrite it in your own words.
    *   God loves you (1 John 4:9–10).

    _____

    *   God is always with you (Hebrews 13:5–6).

    _____

    *   God is at work in your life (Philippians 1:6; 2:13).

    _____

    *   God will give you what you need to do his will (Hebrews 13:20–21).

    _____

2. Fear robs you of the joy in life. Read 1 John 4:18 to find out what God's perfect love does to fear! How does God want you to respond the next time you feel fearful?

    _____

    _____

DAY THREE
Picnic Pals

Hot grilled franks. They're the best. Juicy. Flavorful. There's just nothing like going on a picnic and sinking your teeth into a hot dog! Well, the hot dog and the bun. They are a team. They go hand in hand. The wiener all by its lonesome would be too hot to handle. The bun alone would be dry and sort of tasteless. You have to have the hot dog and bun together. They're buddies.

So are faith and trust. They go together. We have faith that God will work in our lives, according to his plan, even when we can't see it. Believing without seeing—that's faith. We have faith because we trust God's love and faithfulness!

As Christians, God plants a seed of faith in us. That tiny seed grows in two ways. First, the Bible says that faith comes from hearing the Word of God. The Word tells us of God's character (he is loving, just, faithful, righteous, and lots more). It gives us examples of how God has worked in other people's lives. It gives us instruction on specific things God wants us to do. The more we know about God, the more we will surrender our lives to him, knowing he can be trusted. Our faith grows.

The second way our seed of faith sprouts into a plant is by experiencing God firsthand. When we look back and see how God has worked in our lives, it boosts our faith. It assures us of his presence. Maybe he has opened or closed doors to help guide you, or strengthened you when you were ready to quit, or comforted you during a time of sadness. Perhaps he gave you the courage to speak up in class about abstinence when the teacher was talking about the safety

143

of condoms. Or perhaps he gave you the patience you needed to discuss your curfew with your parents.

God is always doing something! When we recognize and acknowledge him, our faith takes root and springs into full bloom. We learn to trust our awesome God, who can do anything! Believing that nothing is impossible with God, then living our life accordingly, proves our faith.

Next time you're in unfamiliar territory and you don't know what to do, pull that faith out of your pocket. Sure, sure, it would be much easier if we knew everything ahead of time. But that wouldn't require any faith.

Hebrews 11:6 tells us that without faith it is impossible to please God. He takes delight in seeing his children believe him and trust him, even when they can't see ahead. Put a smile on his face today. Have faith!

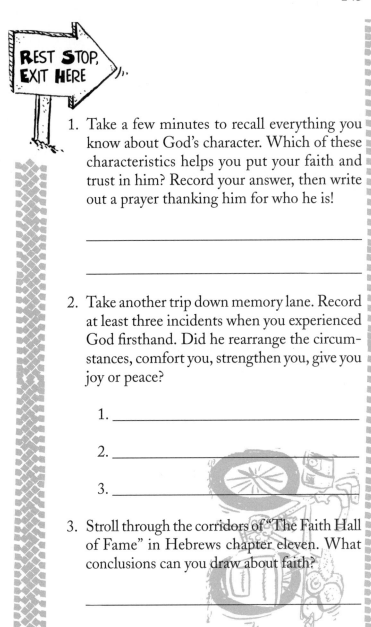

REST STOP, EXIT HERE

1. Take a few minutes to recall everything you know about God's character. Which of these characteristics helps you put your faith and trust in him? Record your answer, then write out a prayer thanking him for who he is!

   _____

   _____

2. Take another trip down memory lane. Record at least three incidents when you experienced God firsthand. Did he rearrange the circumstances, comfort you, strengthen you, give you joy or peace?

   1. _____

   2. _____

   3. _____

3. Stroll through the corridors of "The Faith Hall of Fame" in Hebrews chapter eleven. What conclusions can you draw about faith?

   _____

   _____

DAY FOUR
Slippery When Wet

Geoff could play soccer all day, every day. He made the team at his high school. Problem was, the team wasn't good. Some days Geoff didn't think his teammates even knew where the goal was! So he decided to challenge them by rewarding their next win with a pizza party at his house. Before each game the guys were pumped up and psyched. But it didn't help. They continued to lose.

Leah signed up for private voice lessons through the music department at school. She was even going to get credit for them. After months of learning to breathe correctly, reach high notes, and sustain super-long holds, Leah had made it through the course. So far she had an A. But the instructor was requiring her to perform a solo at the school Christmas program to keep that A. If she didn't do it, she'd get a B. Panic poured all over her. There was no way. She couldn't get up in front of her peers and sing. Leah let fear and inferiority make her decision. She took the B.

Frank woke up tired. Rolling out of bed took all his effort. Even eating his cereal seemed like a chore. Fatigue got the best of him as he decided this day was a downer. He skipped devotions and prayer, heading for campus late. Sharon, the girl who headed up their campus Christian club, stopped him at his locker.

"Frank, I have a makeup exam at lunch today. Could you cover for me at club and do the devotion?" Sharon pleaded.

Frank's fatigue and guilt over skipping his morning time with God got the best of him.

"Gee, Sharon, I can't. God wouldn't want me to do it. Check with Tim."

Emotions! Are they trustworthy? Geoff's enthusiasm didn't result in a winning soccer season. Leah's fear kept her from getting the A she deserved. Frank's sluggish mood and guilty conscience caused him to decide he wasn't God's man for the devotional job.

God doesn't lead us through our emotions. In fact, emotions by themselves are unreliable and often unreasonable. They change continuously: happy, afraid, calm, anxious, confident, depressed, angry, infatuated, impatient.

Emotions and feelings change by the day (ever feel excited at noon and frustrated by dinner?), by the week (ever start off motivated on Monday and fizzled out on Friday?), and by the month (mostly hormone-related stuff). Emotions have high peaks and low valleys. They are like yo-yos!

God might use our emotions to teach us something or to get our attention, but never to direct us! This is especially important to remember when there are unknown curves ahead of you. If you make decisions based on how you feel, failure may await you! Always let things "sit" for a while. Allow time for your emotions to quiet.

Even emotions need to be kept in check with God's word. Is what you are feeling biblical? Is it reasonable? Is it in line with God's character?

When you are praying and discerning God's will, read the Word and listen for God's voice deep within your spirit. Don't let your emotions dictate your actions. Don't trust your feelings. Trust the facts in God's Word.

148

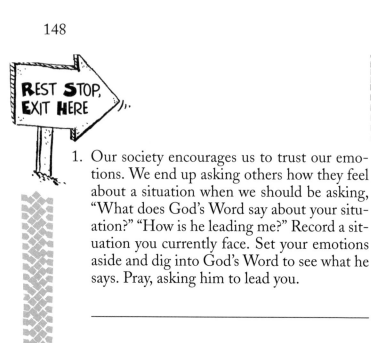

REST STOP, EXIT HERE

1. Our society encourages us to trust our emotions. We end up asking others how they feel about a situation when we should be asking, "What does God's Word say about your situation?" "How is he leading me?" Record a situation you currently face. Set your emotions aside and dig into God's Word to see what he says. Pray, asking him to lead you.

_____

_____

_____

_____

2. Oftentimes we act out of anger. It's one of those strong emotions that can get us in loads of trouble. Record what the following verses teach you about anger: James 1:19–20; Ephesians 4:26; Proverbs 22:24–25.

_____

_____

_____

_____

DAY FIVE
School Crossing

Finally, the day you've dreamed about during those boring history lectures: graduation day. You polish your class ring against the shiny polyester grad gown. It's almost your big moment. Straightening your cap, you walk across the stage. The principal gives your hand a strong shake as you take your diploma. Dad flashes the camera and sighs with relief. Mom wipes the tear from her eye. You reach up to your tassel, moving it from one side to the other. The official declaration of your accomplishment. You did it.

Returning to your seat, the questions, the panic, and the fears rise to form a lump in your throat. WHAT NOW?

The options may seem too big and too varied. You may feel overwhelmed at the idea of what lies around the next curve in your life. Some teens feel all alone in a sea of indecision at that point in their journey.

Fear not! By now you know God has a plan, he's always with you, and he wants you to know what he wants for your life. As you stay close to him and seek him in prayer, he will show you each step.

Back in chapter three you discovered his ultimate goal for your life:

- To become Christlike by developing the character of Jesus—Romans 8:29
- To glorify God in what you say and do—1 Corinthians 6:20; Colossians 3:17
- To tell others how to become part of God's family—Matthew 28:18–20

When it comes to a specific career, prayerfully consider the following:

- What are you naturally good at?
  Has God gifted you in a special area: music, sports, organization, math, science, working with children or the elderly? God-given talents and abilities are often an indication of the direction He wants you to go.

- What are your hobbies and interests?
  It's important to do something you enjoy. Too many people have spent half their lives at jobs they hate (it may pay more or please a parent, but what a drag)!

- What is your definition of success?
  How you answer this question will affect the decisions you make. Do you think fame and fortune are the name of the game, or do character, integrity, and obedience to God rank higher for you?

No matter the profession you hear God calling you to, do it to the best of your ability and for his glory! Your shining example will attract the attention of others. It may open the door for you to share Christ with them. *That* you can do no matter where you work or what you do!

1. John the Baptist was no success in the world's eyes. He lived in the woods, ate locusts, and was beheaded in his early thirties! Yet he had fulfilled God's plan for his life. Do you think God considered his life a success? What kind of sacrifices might you have to make to be a success in God's eyes?

_____

_____

_____

_____

2. Read Luke 12:15–21. What good are a person's possessions when he or she dies? What do you think it means to be rich toward God?

_____

_____

_____

_____

(There's more!)

3. Take some time today to answer each of the
   three questions.

   • What are you naturally good at?

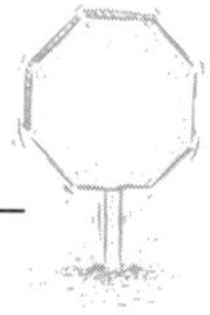

   _____

   _____

   _____

   _____

   _____

   • What are your hobbies and interests?

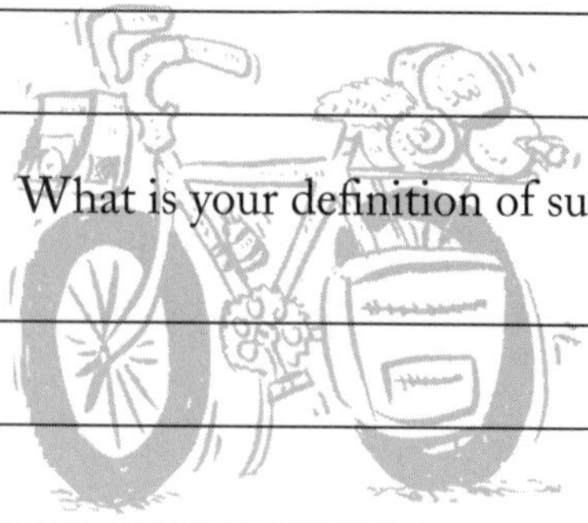

   _____

   _____

   _____

   _____

   • What is your definition of success?

   _____

   _____

   _____

   _____

   _____

Trusting God to speak to you or work in your behalf can leave you weary and speechless! Ever not know what to pray or how to pray? Here are three prayers you can use to hang on while you're waiting on God!

Lord, fill me with the knowledge of your will so I will know what you want me to do and be. Help me to be wise about spiritual things so that I will live in a way that pleases you. Strengthen me with your glorious power so that I can keep going no matter what happens. Help me to always be thankful and joyful in every situation.

Based on Colossians 1:9–12

Heavenly Father, help me to trust you with my whole heart. Keep me from trying to figure everything out, instead of putting my confidence in you. I choose to put you first in all I do and commit my life to you. I delight myself in you, knowing that you have promised to instruct me and guide me along the best pathway for my life.

Based on Proverbs 3:5–6; Psalm 32:8; 37:4–5

Dear God, remind me that you are the Good Shepherd and I am your sheep. As your sheep I hear your voice, and the voice of a stranger I will not obey—only yours. You love me because I am yours and you call me by name as you lead me. Help me to listen for your voice and the gentle nudge of the Holy Spirit. Thank you for protecting me and allowing no one to snatch me out of your hand.

Based on John 10:1–5, 27–28

DETOURS AND DEAD ENDS

Faced with New Decisions

DAY ONE
Bridge Washed Out

Picture it. You've been traveling this road for days. Everything seems to be going along smoothly, when up ahead you see a sign posted and a guardrail set up. Rats. The bridge is out. A detour sign directs you to the left to take the long way around.

Several miles down this new road you notice the colorful wildflowers swaying in the breeze. You notice fish jumping in the stream you would have crossed over. You realize, this is a *better* roadway!

Detours in the road of life usually come as unwelcome setbacks. Who wants to be detained? Who wants to replan their direction? We like to get started and keep going until we get there.

But detours are inevitable. They are bound to happen. God allows them and he makes good use of them. A detour may be one of two things.

154

It could be that you are not really on the right road, so God works to reroute you onto the road he wants you on. In his wisdom he puts up a roadblock and points you to the road he desires.

If you're already on the correct road, a detour may be God's way of redirecting you. It can be his way of getting you to turn to the right or to the left at the perfect time. That's when something happens and you think it is a detour, only to find out down the road it was part of his plan all along!

Joni Eareckson Tada was a young Christian girl who dove into the Chesapeake Bay for an afternoon swim. Her head hit a hard object and snapped back. She felt a weird electric shock in the back of her neck, and her body went numb.

The diving accident left Joni a quadriplegic. Her entire life changed. All the plans she had for herself were gone. Talk about a detour!

Only years later, after a monumental struggle with God over her life in a wheelchair, did Joni recognize God's hand. Today Joni has a huge ministry called Joni and Friends. She helps others who are handicapped maintain their faith and trust in God. She has also recorded several albums, created beautiful artwork using colored pencils clenched between her teeth, and traveled with Billy Graham.

What an incredible detour in Joni's life! God allowed the accident, then he used it to redirect her life.

Your detours may not be as extreme as Joni's. Unexpected intrusions in your life may be moving to a new city, your parents splitting up, someone you love dying, flunking a class, losing your job. They may seem pretty crummy at first, but they may turn out to be blessings in disguise. But no matter what the detour is, our loving Father will continue to direct you on his road for your life. When you face a detour, don't be discouraged. God is just doing a bit of road construction!

REST STOP, EXIT HERE

1. Joni has seen the Lord work in and through her life. She even says she has been able to thank God for her wheelchair! How do you think Joni's life would have been different if she had blamed God and turned away from him?

_____

_____

_____

_____

_____

2. Have you faced detours in your life? List them here, then ask God to use the detours to direct your life in any way he chooses.

_____

_____

_____

_____

_____

DAY TWO
No Thru Traffic

Paul, God's faithful servant, was called to be a preacher. He was chosen to specifically proclaim God's word from city to city.

So what was he doing sitting in a prison in Rome, chained to a big ol' sweaty soldier?

This must have felt like a dead-end road to Paul. In reality, God had stopped him from his travels for a very important reason. It was there, in chains, where Paul wrote letters to churches, giving them guidance and explaining God's principles (Colossians 4:18). Those very letters are what make up most of the New Testament today.

Dead ends can be God's temporary stopping places. He'll slam on the brakes to keep you where he wants you. He has a special purpose for you right there!

Dead ends can also be his way of getting your attention. If you have gotten off the road or have made a string of wrong choices, you may hit bottom. He allows you to come to the end of yourself so that you'll turn back to him. He cares enough about you to intervene!

Balaam was a prophet of God. He was riding on his donkey to the land of Moab where the Lord did not want him to go. While on his way, the donkey veered off the road, then rammed into a wall, smashing Balaam's foot. Then finally the donkey lay down. Balaam was so mad, he struck the donkey each time.

Then the most bizarre thing happened. The donkey spoke! He turned to Balaam and said, "Cool down, buddy! What are you hitting me for? Am I not the best donkey you've ever had?" Balaam replied, "Yeah, yeah. But what's the deal? How come you won't stay on the road?" Right then, an angel of the Lord appeared to Balaam. He had been standing in the middle of the road preventing the donkey from passing by. Balaam hadn't seen the angel, but the donkey had!

God blocked the road because Balaam was on the wrong pathway! God was concerned about Balaam's motives and agenda (Numbers 22).

God used Balaam's donkey to finally get his attention. Dead ends serve as roadblocks that will get our attention, reroute us, or teach us an important lesson.

For Paul, the roadblock was used to temporarily stop his traveling and preaching, allowing him to write. His precious words (directed by the Holy Spirit) not only taught and trained the early church, but they are still speaking to us today.

God intervenes in our lives for his purposes. He loves us and desires the very best for each of his children—even if it means detours and dead ends!

159

1. When you face a dead end in your life, you need new direction. Read Mark 1:35. What did Jesus do? Get all alone with God and listen for his still, small voice.

_____

_____

_____

2. Detours and dead ends are often hard to understand. If we are patient, God may help us to understand. But it's important not to become disappointed or angry and end up hardening our hearts toward the Lord. Read Hebrews 4:16. When you hurt and need help, what two things does God offer? Get a dictionary and define these two words:

Mercy—

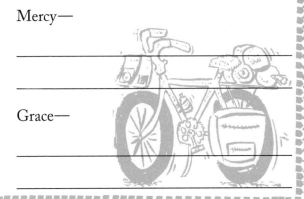

_____

_____

Grace—

_____

_____

DAY THREE
No Parking Anytime

When roadblocks seem to be coming at you from every direction, it can feel overwhelming. Ever want to just pull off the road and park it? Well, quitting is *not* an option! Here is a basic problem-solving plan that can help you sort it all out and keep going. All your life you'll be faced with making decisions and solving problems. No fair trying to run away! Train yourself now to tackle these situations head-on.

The Plan

Step One: Go to the Lord

Start off by asking God for wisdom. He is the one who will ultimately work through these steps to show you his plan. Ask him for whatever else you need as you face this decision, such as peace, patience, courage, or trust.

Step Two: Nail Down the Problem or Dilemma

Identify exactly what the problem is that needs to be solved or the decision that needs to be made. Be honest with yourself about the situation. Now collect the facts about the situation. Don't collect opinions! That can further confuse the issue. Try to determine if it is the situation itself or your interpretation of it that is causing the problem. Next, check a Bible concordance to see what the Scriptures say about your situation.

Step Three: Discover Your Options

Make a list of all your options, both positive and negative. Brainstorm and be creative. Now analyze the list, crossing off those that aren't realistic or aren't in agreement. Put the remaining options in order from best to worst.

Step Four: List the Pros and Cons

One by one, think through each option and record all of its pros and cons. What are the pluses and minuses? What are the possible outcomes of each option? What might the consequences be? How would each option affect you or others involved? Which option would bring glory to God and be a good witness of your faith?

Step Five: Seek Wise Counsel

Now you can get a few opinions from wise, older, and mature Christians. Select Christians you trust and respect. They will be able to help you talk out the situation and the options. It's not a sign of weakness to seek advice. We all need help on our journey.

Step Six: Back to God You Go!

Pray, pray, pray! Offer your situation to the Lord to see what he wants you to do. Quietly wait for his answer. Has your prayer produced an inner feeling of rightness about one of the options? Is God responding with a "go ahead," "wait," or "stop"? Is he showing you a totally new option?

Keep praying day after day until you believe you know what to do. Beware of jumping ahead of God and making hasty decisions.

Step Seven: Act on God's Answer

Having sought the Lord, select the option that best fits his leading. Now step out in faith.

So what are you supposed to do if you have sincerely prayed and followed these steps but still don't know what God is saying? Select the option you truly believe is best. Before you act on it, tell the Lord you are going to go ahead with that option, then ask him to block the way at any time if that action is not his plan.

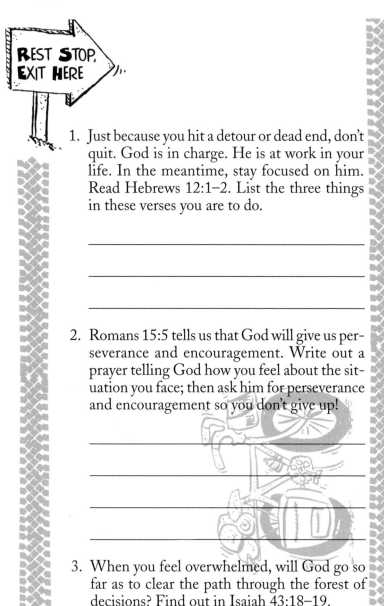

REST STOP, EXIT HERE

1. Just because you hit a detour or dead end, don't quit. God is in charge. He is at work in your life. In the meantime, stay focused on him. Read Hebrews 12:1–2. List the three things in these verses you are to do.

_____

_____

_____

2. Romans 15:5 tells us that God will give us perseverance and encouragement. Write out a prayer telling God how you feel about the situation you face; then ask him for perseverance and encouragement so you don't give up!

_____

_____

_____

_____

3. When you feel overwhelmed, will God go so far as to clear the path through the forest of decisions? Find out in Isaiah 43:18–19.

If You Have a Small
View of God

Your Problems
Will Look
BIG.

If You Have a Big
View of God,

Your Problems
Will Look
small.

DAY FOUR
U-Turns Allowed

There will be times in every Christian's life when he or she doesn't listen to God or doesn't even bother to seek his wisdom before making decisions. He or she may run out of patience and jump ahead of God. Sooner or later, however, that person wakes up to the fact that he has gone the wrong way!

Michael Sweet was rockin' with the band Stryper. He was a talented part of the band's successful CDs and concert tours. But things started rockin' off stage. The group began to leave God out and got into partying. Eventually Sweet was at his lowest point. He left the band. He did a U-turn! He knew he had blown it, gotten way off track. He asked the Lord to forgive him, and he committed himself to following the straight and narrow path that God would lead him down. He made a fresh start—with God and with his music!

Michael had the courage to change directions. That's a tough thing. It means you have to admit you were wrong. You blew it. You may have to eat crow, as they say. You may have to endure embarrassment or peer pressure. The important issue is that you repent and turn around. In the long run, it doesn't matter what others think, but what God thinks. He will give you the courage to make the needed changes! Go to him. Don't let your guilt, regret, or failure drive a wedge between you and God. He knows there will be times you'll blow it. Isn't that the whole reason he provided forgiveness through Jesus? Yes!

Peter was one of the more enthusiastic disciples. He loved Jesus and readily defended him. Remember the garden scene? The soldiers came to get Jesus and Peter drew his sword to stop them.

He took a few swings and cut a guy's ear off (not to worry, Jesus healed him; Luke 22:51)! Peter was the one who walked on the water (Matthew 14:28–31). Peter was the one who pulled Jesus aside to tell him to quit saying he was going to be killed (Matthew 16:16–20). Peter was the one who boldly proclaimed that even if the others denied Jesus, he never would! But Jesus predicted that before the cock crowed Peter would deny him three times.

Oops. Sure enough. By the time the sun came up and the cock let out its cock-a-doodle-do, Peter had said three different times that he didn't know Jesus!

The Bible says he went out and wept bitterly. He couldn't believe what he had done (Luke 22:54–62).

Yet when Jesus had risen from the dead, the angel told Mary to go tell the disciples *and Peter* that Jesus was alive. Jesus specifically wanted Peter to know that he was forgiven.

Jesus offers his forgiveness to each of us. Then he fills us with the strength to "do a U-ie" and turn back toward him. Ask him to help you; he believes in starting over. Second chances. New beginnings. Sometimes it's hard to believe he will forgive us, but he will. That's just part of what makes him so awesome!

1. Pray, asking the Lord to show you if there are roads you need to take a U-turn on. Are you hanging with the wrong friends, dating someone who isn't good for you, partying on the weekends, smoking, lying to your parents, skipping Sunday school? If you need to turn around, ask the Lord to forgive you and show you what you need to do to make changes. Then do it! Don't delay; it will only get harder if you wait.

2. Remember Paul, the guy who wrote lots of the New Testament? He struggled, too. He didn't claim to be perfect. There was something he did, however, to help himself keep going forward. Read Philippians 3:12–14 and record what he did. You can do the same. Don't let past mistakes and failures drag you down. Keep moving ahead in Christ.

_____

_____

_____

_____

_____

DAY FIVE
Priorities Plus

Andrea

I have a personal struggle. It's been going on for years. See, I love to paint. When I was in high school I took lots of art classes. I painted with acrylics back then. I had my easel set up in the basement of our home, in a special corner that had a spotlight above it. I could paint for hours at a time.

It was quiet. Just me, God, and the painting. What fun I had trying to mix the perfect shades of color and create a picture with interest.

In college I switched to watercolors. They have a fresh, delicate look to them. The thing about painting, however, is that practice makes perfect. If I want to be a better painter, I have to invest lots of time. That's where my struggle comes in. I would like to spend more time painting, but it's not a priority to me. There are more valuable ways for me to spend my time.

Time is very precious; therefore, how we spend it is important. What we choose to do with our days and our lives really does matter. One day we will give an account to the Lord for all we have done.

The Bible tells us that only what we do for the Lord is lasting. Only things that have eternal value will remain. Those are the things for which we will be rewarded. So what we do determines whether or not the Lord says to us, "Well done, my good and faithful servant."

That doesn't mean we can't have any fun and just goof off sometimes! And for me, sure, I can take a day now and then to paint. But if that becomes the focus of my life, I won't have much to show for myself when I stand before the Lord. God has not called me to be an artist by profession. It is just a hobby!

I have found that the Lord would rather that I help teach a Bible study, or write notes to those who are struggling with life, write Christian books, visit our sick church members in the hospital, or have lunch with a friend who doesn't know Jesus yet. These are things that will have eternal value for me.

Asking myself the questions *Will this matter at the end of my life?* and *Does this have eternal value?* has helped me make important decisions. They have also helped me set my priorities for life and for each day.

I believe they can help you, also. At the end of your life, it won't matter how big your house was, how many cars you owned, what awards you won, or how much money you earned. It won't matter whether you ever appeared on TV, graced the cover of a magazine, cut your own CD, or won a gold medal.

As Dr. James Dobson puts it, all that will matter in the end is who you loved, who loved you, and what you accomplished for the Lord. Give it some prayerful thought.

Don't Throw Out the Puzzle Before the Pieces Start Fitting Together!

1. Just for fun, put the following list in order according to each act's *eternal* value. One is most valuable, ten is least valuable when compared to the others.

Watch TV all night.
Do chores without being paid.
Offer to babysit your neighbor's kids for free, so their mom can go to Bible study.
Read the latest fashion magazine.
Shoot hoops with an unsaved friend, then tell him or her about Jesus.
Fish every day after school with your brother.
Practice for baseball tryouts.
Collect clothes to be sent to your youth group's Mexico mission project.
Be patient and kind when your brother or sister bugs you.
Bake cookies for your sick friend, then pray for him or her.

See how our answers compare: 9, 6, 2, 10, 1, 7, 8, 5, 4, 3. God first, others second, self last!

2. Read the story of Mary and Martha in Luke 10:38–42. What one thing does Jesus say is most important?

_____

_____

` Traffic Jams

TRAVEL TIPS

If tons of decisions start piling up and running into each other, you're bound to have some fender benders! To help you make more clear-cut decisions, you need goals. Get with God to pray over each area of your life. Then you and the Lord set some goals for yourself.

Whether you are faced with daily decisions (like what to eat, what to wear, when to do your homework, what to do this weekend) or future decisions (like where to go to college, what career to pursue, whom to marry, or where to settle), you can sift through your options and make decisions more effectively if you know your goals!

For Example:

1. If your goal is to be a journalist, which is the better decision?
   A. Work after hours on the school newspaper.
   B. Try out for cheerleading.

2. If your goal is to save money for college, which is the better decision?
   A. Blow thirty bucks on concert tickets and pizza.
   B. Accept that babysitting job.

3. If your goal is to be more Christlike, which is the better decision?
   A. Get up early and go to breakfast Bible study.
   B. Sleep in.

4. If your goal is to have a better relationship with your dad, which is the better decision?
   A. Spend Saturday at the arcade.
   B. Spend Saturday mowing and weeding the yard with your dad.

5. If your goal is to build a healthier body, which is the better decision?
   A. Fast food for lunch and a sundae after school.
   B. Yogurt with fresh fruit and a bag of pretzels after school.

Check your answers: 1. A; 2. B; 3. A; 4. B; 5. B

Get the picture? When you know your goals, decisions will be easier to make! So, here goes. Grab some paper, do some prayin', and then begin to identify your goals in each of the following areas:

Growing in Christ
Church participation
School goals
College goals
Career goals
Fitness and nutritional goals
Financial goals
Relationship goals (parents, siblings, friends)
Others

*You'll never get there
if you don't know
where you are going!*

More Helpful Hints

1. Make "informed decisions" by gathering all the facts and information you can. The more you know, the more educated your decisions will be.

2. Check to see if the decision is irreversible. If so, proceed with caution.

3. Always get your emotions under control before you make decisions. Feelings like anger, fear, jealousy, and momentary exuberance don't lead to smart choices.

4. Ask yourself how the decisions might affect your reputation. Always make choices that uphold your Christianity.

5. In making this decision, are you trying to please someone? If so, who—and why?

6. Tackle one decision at a time, one step at a time. This will prevent you from feeling overwhelmed.

7. Realize that deciding not to decide is a decision. Putting off or avoiding making decisions causes other people or circumstances to decide for you. Avoid this!

8. Determine how a decision might affect your future. Will it lead to peace or confusion? What would Jesus do if he were in your situation?

SIGNAL AHEAD! STOP OR GO?

Submitting to God's Sovereignty

DAY ONE
The Divine Driver

Bill

While I was visiting some members of our church, this sweet little elderly lady told me the pitiful story of her last driving expedition. She had made it safely to the grocery store, but getting in her car to head home turned out to be a disastrous decision. She put the car in gear, preparing to back out of her parking place. But instead of going backwards, the car lunged forward—smack into the car in front of her! Luckily there was hardly any damage to the bumper. She drove home at a turtle speed. Other drivers honked and passed her, increasing her nervousness. As she steered the car into her driveway, she misjudged the angle and heard the crackle of broken flower pots under her wheel. So she let up on the gas and fumbled for the brake. Her foot slipped and she ended up in her front yard! Sounds like a scene from *Driving Miss Daisy!*

Can you imagine riding with this lady? Not me. I'd have white knuckles. I also don't exactly jump at the invitation to ride with most teens. No offense, but some of you are spooky! I'm always a tad nervous and on guard. I can't quite relax, sit back, and enjoy the experience.

How about you? Anyone you're skittish about riding with? Anyone who goes too fast, turns too sharp, weaves in and out between cars like they're in a dodgeball game? That kind of driving doesn't make you feel real safe, right?

There is one person I always feel safe riding with, however. I can kick back and veg out when he's behind the wheel. I know he'll drive with care and caution. I know he won't ever make a wrong turn and end up lost. I know that when I'm cruisin' with him, I'm safe in his hands. That driver is God!

As the passenger, I can totally chill because God is in control. He is sovereign. That means he is the one who ultimately decides when we stop or go, turn left or right, speed up or slow down.

He is sovereign. He is the one who rules and reigns over heaven and earth, even over our lives. Here is how the Scriptures refer to God:

> Mighty One, Faithful, Rock,
> Almighty, Judge, Most High,
> King, Powerful, Holy One

God is the headman! In an army, he's the Commander. In a business, he's the C.E.O. In a ball club, he's the owner *and* head coach.

He is the one in charge! Because of this fact, you and I can tilt back the seat and enjoy the ride. There's no use getting all worked up over every ruffle in our lives! We're not in control anyway. God alone is sovereign!

1. Understanding God's sovereignty plays a major part in living the Christian life. Think through these verses: Psalm 103:19; 1 Chronicles 29:11; Daniel 4:34–35. Now round up your dictionary and look up *sovereign*. Next, in your own words, write a definition of God's sovereignty.

_____

_____

2. Keep that dictionary busy today. There are three words that refer to God's sovereignty. Define each one:

Omniscient—

_____

Omnipotent—

_____

Omnipresent—

_____

Take a moment to thank God for always being with you, always knowing the details of your life, and for being powerful enough to be in control.

DAY TWO
Under Construction

A clump of hard, cold clay. Sitting there on its own, it doesn't have much use or appeal. Oh, you can find it in a variety of dull shades like stony gray, dirt brown, or brick red. Other than that, there's not much to it. Unless you're a potter. Now, that guy can look at a lump of clay and see all sorts of possibilities: a cup, a vase, a bowl.

The potter chooses the type of pottery he wants to create from the clay. He has a specific purpose already planned. And a specific design. The potter plans the shape that will best fill the use of the pottery. He decides on the appropriate pattern for perfect eye appeal. Then he chooses the colors he will carefully glaze onto the clay creation.

With the finished product in mind, the real work begins. The potter firmly throws the clay into the center of his potter's wheel. Then his water-dipped hands prepare to mold the clay. The potter works the clay to make it soft and responsive to the pressure he applies as he forms the shape. He removes any impurities that might mar his precious pottery.

After the laborious process is complete, the potter is pleased. He takes great pride in each of his one-of-a-kind creations. What started as a lump of hard clay becomes valuable in the hands of the potter. It can now be used for the purpose the potter planned.

Several places in the Bible God is called the Potter; we are the clay. He is the one who decides the purpose for our lives. He brings circumstances and trials—the ups and the downs—in order to remove our impurities and soften us.

176

In his hands we become moldable as he works toward the finished product he has in mind.

The things we experience all have a purpose. They are part of God's molding process. Each event is calculated. This may be hard to accept when you hurt, feel cheated, or appear trapped. But be patient. God is working! You are being molded into perfect shape!

God's ultimate design for you is to be like Jesus. He's molding you into the image of his Son. You are still unfinished. Yet, like clay, you must choose to remain in the Potter's hands, always ready to be molded for his purpose and pleasure.

REST STOP, EXIT HERE

1. Knowing our sovereign God is working in and through the circumstances of our lives is very comforting. It gives us the courage to say, "everything will work out the way God has planned." How does this truth affect your outlook on life? Share this truth today with someone who needs encouragement.

2. Read Romans 9:20–21. Do you ever want to ask God what he's doing? Why life seems wacky? Why he's making you into a cup when you wanted to be a vase? He may never answer, but in the meantime, keep a check on your attitudes. Which of the following will help you stay moldable?

   Demanding your way . . . or realizing God's in charge
   Obeying God's Word . . . or rebelling against God's ways
   Jealousy and envy . . . or contentment with what God has given you
   Impatience . . . or waiting for God's timing
   Trusting God's wisdom . . . or worry and fear

DAY THREE
Between Stop and Go

Traffic signals are great. They keep the flow of cars going in an orderly fashion. Without them, there would be total confusion, and a few crashes, too!

God's Word, like traffic signals, gives us direction. Sometimes when we pray about which road to follow, we get a green light: GO. Other times it's red: STOP. Very often we get a yellow: WAIT. Stop and go are pretty easy to understand. But yellow, that's a tricky one.

Does God want you to proceed with caution or prepare to stop?

Maybe he wants you to stay where you are and wait for his timing or his clear direction.

Waiting on the Lord is more than being stuck somewhere between stop and go. It's not the land of limbo! It's not time to kick back and get comfy. Waiting on the Lord is not a time to do nothing. It's not passive, it's active!

Here are some *active* steps for you to take while you wait for God to clear your path, give you direction, or answer your prayers.

1. *Pray.* Bring your requests or situation before the Lord every day. Pursue an answer with diligence. Ask God to show you his purpose, his timing, and his way of doing things.
   Ask, seek, knock (Matthew 7:7–8).

2. *Read.* Start with the Bible. Get into God's presence and find out what the Word says about your situation. Observe how God worked in the lives of Bible

179

characters. Read Christian books that relate to whatever you are waiting for.

God's Word is a light to your path (Psalm 119:105).

3. *Watch.* Expect God to do something. Maybe he needs to rearrange your circumstances or change your attitude before he can move you ahead.

Eagerly watch and wait expectantly (Psalm 5:3).

4. *Be patient.* Beware of running ahead of God! Resist the desire to devise a backup plan in case God doesn't come through—he will! No grumbling or complaining. Trust him! He knows what he's doing.

Receive God's promises through faith and patience (Hebrews 6:12).

5. *Don't quit.* Use waiting periods to grow closer to God. Let his divine power recharge your battery. He will keep you keepin' on.

God renews your strength when you wait (Isaiah 40:31).

6. *Listen.* Don't turn down the sound just because you're in God's waiting room. Now's the time to tune in. God is faithful. He will eventually speak to you. Keep doing the last thing he told you to do until he gives you something new.

Speak, Lord, for your servant is listening (1 Samuel 3:9).

*Actively
Wait
for God!*

1. When you are in God's Waiting Room, you may be tempted to misinterpret his silence. Don't buy Satan's lies! Read these portions of Scripture and discover the truth.

Satan's Lie	God's Truth
God is not listening to me	1 John 5:14–15; 1 Peter 3:12
God must not love me	Romans 8:38–39; John 3:16
God has forgotten about me	Isaiah 49:15–16

2. Waiting on God does have positive results. Waiting gives you new strength. It teaches you to depend on God and to know him more intimately. Plus, when God does answer, you'll have increased confidence. List other positive results:

_____

_____

_____

_____

3. Pray, thanking God for each of these!

DAY FOUR
Super Shock Absorbers

Hardly anyone knew his name, but every day, there he was, lying against the temple gate. Someone had obviously placed him there. He had been crippled since birth—unable to walk and move around on his own. He didn't head off to work every morning like the other men; he couldn't. So he begged, just to stay alive.

On that particular day, Peter and John were headed into the temple to pray. Seizing every opportunity, the crippled man called out to them, asking for money. Peter and John stopped. The man looked up at them, expecting some coins. That's not what he got.

"We don't have any money for you! But I'll give you something else! I command you in the name of Jesus Christ of Nazareth, *walk!*" (Acts 3:6).

At that instant, Peter reached down and took the cripple by the hand and pulled him to his feet. Immediately the man's feet and ankles were made strong! He jumped up and started walking! He could hardly believe it. He praised God with shouts of joy!

Imagine it. The guy was expecting money but got a miracle. He expected a few coins but got a new chance at life.

That's the weird thing about our expectations. They get us looking for a particular thing to happen. We decide how something should turn out. We get our minds set on it. Then God moves in and—BAM!—he does something totally different (but always better).

Too many expectations can leave you feeling disappointed, maybe even frustrated, that things didn't work out the way you thought they would. Why not replace those fickle expectations with faith-filled flexibility?

A flexible attitude, like shock absorbers, will make your ride through life less bumpy. A flexible attitude will keep you calm and patient. You'll be more content knowing God is in control. Flexibility helps you go with the flow. It's a pathway to peace.

When you're a flexible kind of guy or gal, you can confidently offer yourself to the Lord. You have the courage to give God a blank writing pad and say, "Here you go, God. You write down the plans for my life." That's allowing God to live through you.

A flexible attitude is accepting the fact that Jesus is Lord. Not you, him! A flexible attitude says, "Hey, I gave my life to Jesus, now he can do what he wants with it!" He can change it, interrupt it, turn it left, turn it right—whatever he wants.

Be flexible with the Lord. *Do* expect him to work in your life. *Don't* expect him to do it your way. He is Lord!

> *Whatever God leads you into,*
> *he will lead you out of!*

REST STOP, EXIT HERE

1. Proverbs 27:1 (NASB) says, "Do not boast about tomorrow, for you do not know what a day may bring forth." Only God knows what is ahead for you. How can this help you stay flexible?

   _____

   _____

2. What expectations are you carrying around? Are they setting you up for disappointment? Are they limiting God? List them here; then give them to the Lord.

   a. _____

   b. _____

   c. _____

   d. _____

3. Write a prayer to God, offering your life as a blank writing pad, inviting him to do what he wants with your life.

   _____

   _____

DAY FIVE
Map Maker

Andrea

The Atlantic City convention center rocked with thunderous applause as Miss America 1995 was announced. The judges had selected an amazing young woman from Alabama named Heather Whitestone. She amazed them with her grace and charm. Amazed them with her encouragement to youth. And amazed them with her inspiring ballet performance. She especially amazed them because she was deaf.

Heather had suffered a rare reaction to a childhood vaccination when she was just eighteen months old. The medicine that saved her life left her deaf!

During her high school years, Heather really struggled with being deaf. She prayed that God would allow her to hear again. But that was not his choice for her. Through the Bible, God showed Heather that he has a reason for everything and that she could trust him.

Eventually Heather made peace with God's sovereign plan. When I interviewed Heather for a *Brio* article, she shared, "I told God I don't choose to be deaf, but if he can use my deafness to change other people's lives, then I will be deaf for him." She went on to say that she knew that if she had turned away from God in anger and bitterness, she may never have been crowned Miss America.

Heather's life is a perfect example of God's sovereignty. He allowed her deafness in order for her to be a powerful witness for him. It was his plan for Heather to be deaf. It was his plan for Heather to be Miss America.

Heather's response is an example for each of us. She accepted God's plan and allowed him to use her life as he desired.

Accepting God's sovereignty. Being flexible to his plan. Staying moldable in his hands. Saying "yes" to the things he brings into your life. Each of these are vital if you are truly seeking God's direction for your life.

If you say no to God and dig in your heels against him, you'll have no peace. You'll end up being bitter and resentful. The love relationship God desires with you will rot away.

It's true that you won't understand everything our sovereign God allows or directs you to do. You won't like everything, either. Yet other things will bring you great joy and gratitude. Your life will overflow with a peace you never thought possible.

Everything God allows in your life is another thread he is using to weave an incredible design. Every detour, crossroad, traffic jam, U-turn, dangerous curve, bridge, exit ramp, highway, or country road will be part of the map God is using to get you where he wants you.

He knows the plan. He will reveal it to you, step by step, as you stay close to him. Discovering God's will is a continual journey. Trust him. We know you'll have a great trip!

1. Meditate on this statement:

    Nothing comes into your life that hasn't first
    filtered through God's fingers of love.

    Who is ultimately in control? Does God sift
    through the events of life, allowing some and
    blocking others? What is his motive? Ex-
    plain how the statement above can bring you
    comfort.

    _____

    _____

    _____

    _____

2. We serve a God "who by his mighty power at
    work within us is able to do far more than we
    would ever dare to ask or even dream of—
    infinitely beyond our highest prayers, desires,
    thoughts or hopes" (Ephesians 3:20). God, the
    ruler of all things, has a plan for your life. It is
    far better than you could plan for yourself!
    Trust his sovereignty!

Jesus Is Lord of *All*

or

He's Not Lord at *All*

He's not a part-time God!

(For Your
Information)

Be still and know that I am God.
Psalm 46:10 NIV

The Lord has established His throne
in the heavens;
And His sovereignty rules over all.
Psalm 103:19 NASB

And don't forget the many times I
clearly told you what was going to
happen in the future. For I am God—
I only—and there is no other like me
who can tell you what is going to hap-
pen. All I say will come to pass, for I do whatever I wish.
Isaiah 46:9–10

My soul, wait in silence for God only,
For my hope is from Him.
Psalm 62:5 NASB

Wait for the LORD;
Be strong, and let your heart take courage;
Yes, wait for the LORD.
Psalm 27:14 NASB

Yet those who wait for the LORD
Will gain new strength;
They will mount up with wings like eagles,
They will run and not get tired,
They will walk and not become weary.
Isaiah 40:31 NASB

Do not fear, for I am with you;
Do not anxiously look about you, for I am your God.
I will strengthen you, surely I will help you,
Surely I will uphold you with My righteous right hand.
Isaiah 41:10 NASB

THE REARVIEW MIRROR

Looking back over our lives, we can see how God has directed us, even when we were unaware of it.

Because God is sovereign, you can trust him to be at work in your life even when you can't see his plan at that time. In some cases, you won't be able to clearly identify how he has directed you until you can check the rearview mirror of life and look back. Like they say, hindsight is 20/20!

Discovering God's direction in your life is a journey. It's a process. He does speak to his children. Keep uncovering his general will in his Word. Listen for his specific will as you develop that intimate, loving relationship with him. Above all else, don't ever give up or let go of God. Continue to ask, seek, and knock. In his timing, he will answer and show you the way!

Andrea and Bill Stephens are members of the Covington Presbyterian Church, Covington, Louisiana, where Bill is pastor. Andrea is beauty editor of *Brio* magazine, published by Focus on the Family. She often speaks at women and youth conferences and retreats.

You Can Invite Andrea Stephens
to Speak at Your Next
Youth Conference
or Retreat!

Seminars Available:
I'm Glad You Know Where We're Going, Lord!
Discovering God's direction in your life.

God Thinks You're a Babe!
Teaching girls to love their looks!

You Want Me to W-W-W-W-Witness?
Learn how easy it is to tell others about Christ every day!

Being God's Kid in a Tough Teen World
Uncover the secret of putting God first
in four important areas of your life!

Stressed Out, but Hangin' Tough!
Find out God's answer for handling stress,
plus tons of practical tips!

The Importance of Being You!
Learn how to boost your self-esteem and appreciate your
unique personality, gifts, and talents!

Glamour to Glory
From Model to Minister's Wife!
Andrea Stephens's personal testimony.

For more information contact:

Andrea Stephens
P.O. Box 5926
Glen Allen, VA 23058